# Lean Transformation:
## How to Change Your Business into a Lean Enterprise

# About the Authors:

**Bruce A. Henderson** is Chief Executive of Invensys Controls, a unit of Invensys plc. Mr. Henderson's group, the world's largest manufacturer of controls for home and commercial HVAC systems and appliances, is a $3.2 billion company. His organization employs more than 30,000 people, and has more than 100 plants located in 16 countries. Mr. Henderson holds two bachelor degrees from Brown University, one in electrical engineering and the other in political science, and an MBA from Wharton School of Business. A former McKinsey & Company consultant, he also ran several businesses for TRW, where he became a proponent of lean enterprise through his experience supplying Toyota manufacturing facilities.

**Jorge L. Larco** is uniquely qualified to help companies large or small, multinational or regional, transform into lean enterprises wherever they may be located. Born in Argentina, a U.S. Citizen by choice, Mr. Larco speaks English, Spanish, French, and Italian fluently, and is able to conduct business in Portuguese. He has successfully led conversions to lean in locations such as Italy, France, Brazil, the United Kingdom, Australia, New Zealand, and the United States. A graduate of the Tuck Executive Program of The Amos Tuck Schoolof Business Administration  at Dartmouth, he also holds an M.S. degree in electromechanical and electronic engineering from the University of Buenos Aires, and is a former general manager of TRW operations in Pamplona, Spain.

# Lean Transformation:
## How to Change Your Business
## into a Lean Enterprise

by

Bruce A. Henderson and Jorge L. Larco

**THE OAKLEA PRESS**
RICHMOND, VIRGINIA

FIRST EDITION
Fifth Printing, November 2000

ISBN 0-9646601-2-1

If your bookseller does not have this book in stock, it can be ordered directly from the publisher. More information, including a discount schedule for quantity purchases, can be found at the Web site given below.

The Oaklea Press
P.O. Box 29334
Richmond, VA 23242-0334

Voice: 1-800-295-4066
Facsimile: 1-804-784-2852
Email: OakleaPres@aol.com

Web site: http://www.LeanTransformation.com

We dedicate this book to our wives,
Mary Henderson and Silvia Larco,
without whose support and patience
this book could not have been.

# Acknowledgements

We'd like to thank our editor, publisher, and friend, Stephen Hawley Martin, without whose help and effort this book would not have been written and published. Steve worked long and hard to make it a reality.

We'd like to extend our thanks to John Sharood, of Invensys Controls in Richmond, Virginia, for his contribution to the discussion under the heading "Finance" in Part III, and to Martin Beyer, also of Invensys Controls in Richmond for his help with many of the graphs and charts throughout the book. Luiz Silveira of Invensys Appliance Controls, Caxias, Brazil, contributed practical advice and helpful insights employed throughout the book and deserves special thanks. We are also grateful in this regard to Jim Mueller, Chief Operating Officer of Invensys plc in London, and to Elena Bortolan of Invensys Climate Controls, Belluno, Italy. Each read an early draft and provided constructive criticism, pointers, anecdotes, and encouragement.

Allen M. Yurko, Chief Executive of Invensys plc, deserves special recognition for his drive to make "Lean" an integral part of Invensys' strategy. Allen's support throughout this program has been crucial to its success.

And finally, we'd like to thank Dr. James P. Womack, one of the world's leading experts in lean thinking, who graciously reviewed this book while it was still a fledgling manuscript. Jim provided many positive suggestions, helpful feedback, and important critical analysis. His thoughts concerning what we have written are reflected in the foreword.

This book, like all true lean enterprises, is the result of an empowered team effort.

# CONTENTS

**Foreword**

**Preface**

# CONTENTS, Continued

## PART III, The Lean Enterprise, Spreading Lean Throughout

## PART IV, Sustaining the Change

# Foreword

By

James P. Womack
President
Lean Enterprise Institute

*Lean Transformation* is a leading indicator of a profound change in our business culture. Bruce Henderson started his career as a strategy consultant seeking to position businesses so they faced the minimum of competition. Jorge Larco began his business life as an operations manager running plants in a traditional manner. In a previous era they would have had no cause to talk to each other because strategists advising CEOs did not consider operations important and because operating managers lacked a strategic vision for the business extending beyond the walls of their plant. Today—after what they describe as a trip to Toyota boot camp—they are not only talking. They have jointly written a book on how to make lean operations the key strategy for businesses large and small. What's going on here?

The answer, I think, is that in a globalized economy with many mature industries it's impossible to avoid competition and critically important to answer a simple question: How can managers create value for customers by eliminating waste in routine operations in plants, engineering, purchasing, distribution, and retail. This is not to say that positional strategies are irrelevant—Henderson's company has just consummated a gigantic merger to strengthen its position in several industries. It is to say that mere position is no longer sufficient. The list of mergers that have failed to produce their promised "synergies" due to lack of a lean operating plan is now very long. And down-stream customers, including you and me as ultimate consumers, are placing steadily higher demands on businesses to cut out the waste and perform. The strategists and business raiders of the 1980s have therefore given way to the new business hero of the late 1990s—Michael Dell—who has created one of the world's most successful companies by eliminating wasted steps (like the retailer) and installing build-to-order pull systems to give people just what they want just when they want it.

In the pages of *Lean Transformation* the authors describe a simple method for making a Dell out of your business, beginning with high-level leadership initiatives to refocus the business, then quickly getting to the down-and-dirty steps needed to transform operations. After a careful reading of this fast-paced text, I hope CEOs will finally get it: Waste can only be eliminated and value created if you pay close attention to every action currently consuming your resources. Ask what's waste and what's value for the end customer, then eliminate the waste. And I hope operations managers will also get it: Brilliant operations employing lean principles is your company's smartest strategy almost without respect to the business you are in. Read *Lean Transformation*, take notes, screw up your courage, and then explain the new reality to your CEO!

I hope the readers of *Lean Transformation*—both CEOs and operations managers—will be at the forefront of the worldwide effort to transform lean thinking from a leading-edge concept into the standard operating practice in every industry. I'm certain the lean thinkers will win before we get very far into the new millennium and I advise the reader to heed Henderson and Larco's warning: If your firm starts down the lean path first you can always stay ahead but if you start later you may find it impossible to catch up!

# Preface

Leaders of companies today face a critical choice. They can be content with the status quo, or they can lead their businesses into a new era in which lean enterprise will be the norm. If they are first in their field, we believe they will reap tremendous benefits. If they allow their competitors a head start, they will find themselves in the position of playing catch up. In either case, we believe the time required to read this book will be time well spent. For those planning to transform to lean, it should provide insight and direction. For those planning to wait and see, it will give knowledge of what they may be up against.

This is not, of course, the only book that has been written on lean enterprise, nor is it the only one a serious student of the subject should read and study. Perhaps the most significant is *The Machine That Changed The World*, published in 1990, and written by James P. Womack, Daniel T. Jones, and Daniel Roos. It focuses on the automobile industry and offers profound insights into the methods employed by Toyota—methods which make that company the most efficient, and certainly one of the highest quality automobile manufacturers in the world.

Dr. Womack and Professor Jones followed that groundbreaking work in 1996 with *Lean Thinking,* a volume that carries further lean concepts first presented in their earlier work to explore how they can be applied to the benefit of practically any business or industry.

It is not our intention to replicate what has already been written. Rather, we believe we can make valuable additions to the published body of knowledge on this subject. Between the two of us, we process more than twenty years of practical experience in taking companies lean. This experience spans the globe, from North and South America, to Europe, India, China, and the Pacific Rim.

Our education began at Toyota boot camp, but what we have encountered since may prove more valuable to you. It is something few Toyota executives possess: extensive experience in transforming organizations to lean that had previously been steeped in the methods, practices, and mind sets of traditional mass producers. Experts in the field generally agree that transforming a traditional company into a lean enterprise is considerably more difficult than starting one from scratch. With this in mind, we believe that the knowledge we will share will be instructive and valuable to others following this route.

Settle back as we share our experiences, point out pitfalls, and show the way around obstacles we've encountered along the way. Whether your business is small, or a worldwide leader, it is our hope that by conveying to you what we have learned, we will help further the success of your lean transformation.

# PART I

# Lean Enterprise as Business Strategy

Let's say you're a CEO, or perhaps a business owner. Imagine your company is the leader of its industry with market share that comfortably exceeds your nearest competitor. You have the industry's shortest manufacturing lead time for your products—five weeks; you have 99% good quality; and you hardly ever miss a delivery date that you told a customer you'd achieve. You make a pretty good profit. Though you aren't necessarily the lowest-cost producer, no one can deny you hold the top position in the market. All in all, life is good.

One day, your head of marketing tells you that the Number Two competitor ("Yes," you think, "that *distant* Number Two") has just been acquired. The new owners, you are told, have had some success with their acquisitions in other industries—touting something called "lean enterprise." They are new to your industry, so naturally, you feel secure in believing these upstarts are not to be taken seriously.

For several months, you don't hear much about the "new" company, which strengthens your conviction that your initial instincts were correct. Then one day (a Friday afternoon, naturally) your head of marketing bursts into your office with the news that you have just lost a critical customer order to Number Two. The upstart has lowered its prices 10% below yours, quoted one-week lead time to the customer's *desired* delivery date, and guaranteed 99.9% quality!

You're appalled, of course, that this company would buy business like this. You decide not to match the price, knowing that your competitor cannot sustain a loss-making business. You console your marketing chief, and go back to business as usual.

A few more months go by. Things are not so comfortable as they used to be. Your company is now losing customer orders left and right. Prices have eroded 5-10%, cutting deeply into margins; your factory is in chaos because of shorter lead times being demanded by the customers; and your once-vaunted quality levels have slipped terribly. As if this weren't bad enough, Number Two has just reduced order lead times to a single day, and is touting "six sigma" quality (essentially zero defects). You hear that it is about to gobble up the Number Three competitor and combine that business into its original plant. In addition, they're now introducing new products every six months compared to your 12 to 18 month cycle.

Does this scenario sound far fetched? It isn't. It is standard fare for a competitor that successfully implements lean enterprise. Your competitor has been transformed from a sleepy snail into something more like a sleek and cunning jaguar—stealthily approaching its prey, and then bringing it down with a ferocious, lightning-fast attack.

What if you indeed have a truly world class competitor on your hands? This is a company with a manufacturing lead time of four hours, virtually defect-free products, and rarely missed delivery. This competitor is fiercely price competitive and has new product development and introduction times that are measured in months. Not possible? Most of Toyota's leading suppliers have performed at this level for years.

The question is, would you be able to compete? Probably not if you continue using traditional mass production methods of operation. This is why we say that lean enterprise is strategic; it is not a tactical operations improvement program.

Lean enterprise is an alternative approach your company can take that will make life extremely difficult for your competition. You could be the first in your industry to become a truly lean producer—and to reap the benefits of the success this will bring, rather than allowing someone else to do so. Imagine what you could do if your productivity went up by 25-40%, and if you could free up nearly half the floor space in your factories. Suppose your inventory was reduced by two-thirds (or more), and that you could run circles around your competitors with respect to lead time and quality.

How much market share could you gain? What could you do with the extra profit and cash flow? Would you lower prices, or just put more profit on the bottom line?

Let's look at a real life example. For the 1997 model year, Toyota introduced a new Camry priced $600 more than its previous model. At the beginning of that same model year, Ford introduced a newly designed Taurus intended to compete against the Camry. The new Taurus cost almost *$1,000* more than the old one. The new Camry started at around $16,700; the Taurus at more than $18,000.[1] The following model year, Toyota was able to *lower* the Camry's cost by $350. Ford *increased* the cost of the Taurus by $385,[2] creating an even larger cost differential. With pricing like this, it doesn't take a wizard to predict which is likely to win the car wars.

## Toyota, the Leader in Lean Enterprise

Toyota cars and trucks are known for quality and dependability, which no doubt has been a major factor in that company's success in the U.S. market. It is not a coincidence that Toyota pioneered the techniques we will be discussing.

American automobile manufacturers have been slow to adopt lean enterprise, and the consequences are apparent in the sales history of this nation's largest auto maker. During the time that Toyota built a positive reputation and attendant market share, the share enjoyed by General Motors cars and trucks declined dramatically. GM's portion of the business has plummeted from almost 60% in the early 1960s to a figure of 28.4% as of this writing. This is the lowest since 1926 when GM had only 26% of the market.[3]

Lean enterprise generally receives credit as the agent behind Toyota's outstanding record of quality products. But lean techniques lead to much more than high quality. As lean producers get better at what they do, their costs go down. For Toyota, they resulted in a new Camry that cost less to make, even though the company has been practicing lean enterprise for almost fifty years. The beginning of lean enterprise dates, by the way, to 1950 when a young Japanese engineer named Eiji Toyoda[4] spent three months studying Ford's Rouge plant in Detroit. Mr. Toyoda learned Ford's methods and thought of ways to improve upon them. He did so by keeping a keen eye out for waste, or *muda*, as any kind of wasted motion, effort, or materials is known in Japanese. A basic tenet of the Toyota method, and therefore of lean enterprise, is to eliminate activities that do not add value for the end user of a product or service. Another is continually to look for and implement improvements in the process. This is what Toyota has been up to. That company's experience is proof that perfection can be approached, but never reached. Toyota just keeps on getting better and more efficient at making cars.

## Lean Enterprise, the Big Gun in Your Arsenal

Let's look at a couple of case studies of effective lean strategies—Vanguard Burger, a fictitious fast food store, and Dell Computer, a real life success story.

Imagine, for example, that the time normally required from order to delivery in your industry is measured in weeks. Now, suppose that you're able to cut this to a day or two, perhaps even to a matter of hours, and that you can do it without increasing inventory. (You actually will be able to reduce inventory dramatically.)

How? You institute continuous flow manufacturing, a technique we will be discussing in depth. For the moment, simply imagine you set up your plant like the kitchen of a Wendy's restaurant, or a Subway Sandwich Shop, in which a food order is not assembled until a customer appears at a cash register and says exactly what he or she wants.

As each order is placed at Vanguard Burger, it appears instantly where workers can see it. Let's say that an order is coming in now that is the equivalent in your industry of a deluxe quarter pound hamburger without onions.

A hamburger is removed from the grill, where it has just finished cooking, and placed on a bun. Your workers do not miss a beat as the burger moves from one to another. They place just the right ingredients picked from strategically located bins of lettuce, pickle, tomatoes, mustard, ketchup, mayonnaise and hold the onions. When the finished hamburger arrives at the end of the line, it is packaged for the customer—warm and ready to eat.

Let's say this order came at the expense of a competitor who was unable to give the customer exactly what he or she wanted. Oh, your competitor had plenty of quarter pound hamburgers in stock. More than enough. The problem was that he didn't have one on hand without the onions. So, he was not in position to deliver, unless the customer was willing to wait.

Why should it take so long?

Rather than continuous flow to customer pull, your competitor operates in the batch-and-queue mode employed by many fast food rivals of the restaurants listed. Burgers are cranked out rapid fire and piled in huge holding bins, ready to ship. Tons of burgers are ready and waiting, a big pile of them smoldering under a hot light. Some with cheese and some without. Some with sauce and some with no sauce. With pickles and without. But at present, every combination also has onions. And the no-onion variety isn't scheduled to run until later in the day.

At first, when your competitor loses the sale, he thinks nothing

## Figure 1.1

### Lean Enterprises Have Strategic Advantage

| | |
|---|---|
| Manufacturing lead time | < 1 day |
| Delivered Quality | 3 PPM |
| Delivery Performance | 99+% |
| Inventory Turns | > 50 |
| Conversion Cost (materials to finished goods) | 25-40% less than mass producers |
| Manufacturing space | 35-50% less than mass producers |
| New product development | < 6 months |

of it. Oh, well, all out of quarter pound hamburgers without onions. Couldn't give Charlie what he wanted today, so he's headed down the street. These things happen. He'll be back.

But now Charlie has been spoiled. He's seen how your company can deliver. Fresh, hot and just the way he likes his burgers. He's impressed. He decides he'll try your outfit again. This time he wants a grilled chicken sandwich, but not just any, standard-make grilled chicken sandwich. He wants one without pickles and with double tomatoes. Your workers swing into action. You deliver. Charlie is impressed.

Now Charlie wants a fish sandwich. He comes to you again.

You deliver. Charlie is pleased. He likes them hot, and he likes them just the way he likes them. So he comes again, this time for a breakfast burrito.

You deliver.

You get his business again. And again. And now it's not just Charlie's business that you get. The word is out. Customers begin moving to you and away from your competitor in droves. Your competitor suddenly realizes he's got to do something, or face the prospect of going out of business. He's up to his ears in burgers with everything on them including onions. He's got a whole bin full of fully-loaded grilled chicken sandwiches baking under the light. Fish sandwiches are overflowing the warming ovens. But he hardly ever seems to have precisely what his customers ask for.

Put yourself in this competitor's shoes. We'll call him Frank. How would you expect Frank to respond?

## Why Competitors Will Have Difficulty Copying You

If he holds true to form, even if he knows how you are able to customize your orders (the Vanguard Burger method), Frank isn't likely to copy you. His vice president of manufacturing will have a bunch of reasons right off the top of his head why continuous flow won't work in his particular situation. These will range from the assumption that the continuous flow method is inefficient (an incorrect assumption) to arguments that his equipment isn't designed for it. It's high speed equipment not timed for continuous flow. Each machine cost the company millions, but for good reason. Each can crank out 365 quarter pound burgers a second. The same machines can knock out 842 fish sandwiches before you can say Jack Sprat. (Of course, it takes quite a while to change the set up from burgers to fish sandwiches.) Yes indeed, this high speed equipment is not only a major asset depreciating on the balance sheet, it is state-of-the-art. What a waste it would be to slow it down to the snail's pace of assembly line workers. And besides, the plant is not laid out for continuous flow. The workers won't stand for it. Accounting practices aren't set up for it, and on and on and on it will go.

Perhaps our man Frank argues with his VP manufacturing, and when this doesn't work, Frank tells him at least to give it a try. After all, who needs 365 burgers without onions if they can only sell four? The VP manufacturing, not wanting to lose his job, says he'll think seriously about ways it might be done.

But it isn't long before others in the organization come to the VP manufacturing's defense. Listen, Frank, they say. We aren't objecting to lean enterprise because we've heard that it means flattening out the organization. And certainly not because it calls for decision-making that is closer to the customer; closer to the problems; closer to people who know what's really going on and how to fix things. We're all for teamwork, yes-sir-ree. We don't mind giving up some authority. Not in the least.

Then they list a thousand reasons lean enterprise is not a good idea for the particular company Frank runs. Our situation is different, they say. It's unique. We tried something like it once before and it was a disaster. Lean enterprise might work over at Vanguard Burger, but it will never work here.

Poor Frank. What's he going to do?

## How Batch and Queue Can Lead to Ruin

As long as he sticks with the batch-and-queue method of doing business, he only has one way to go. He'll have to increase inventory. He'll crank out burgers and grilled chicken and fish sandwiches in an ever increasing range of varieties. That VP manufacturing will have those high speed machines working overtime. He'll have his workers stacking breakfast burritos and bacon and egg biscuits to the ceiling in holding bins with bright, hot lights on them. The objective will be to have on hand whatever a customer wants so that it can be shipped immediately.

Of course, the company's cash will be depleted, but Frank does not have any choice. Not if he's going to compete using batch and queue. Vanguard Burger has spoiled the customer base with their continuous flow to customer demand method of doing business. Customers are no longer willing to take its sandwiches the way Frank makes them, or wait for a new run to take place. Building inventory is the only option Frank has. Otherwise, he simply cannot meet customer needs.

And surely the cash crunch will come. Frank won't have any more room to stack hamburgers, grilled chicken sandwiches, cheeseburgers and breakfast burritos. He'll have a sale to reduce that excess inventory before it's so soggy and tasteless that every penny is lost.

Inevitably, Frank's profits will plummet. Shareholders will be up in arms. After a year or two, or maybe a few quarters of getting beaten up, Frank may come to you to ask if Vanguard Burger would like to buy this once staunch competitor.

Sure, maybe, you tell him, if the price is right. And, Frank, if we do buy your company, hold the holding bins and that expensive high speed equipment that doesn't make sense with continuous flow to customer pull. And we're not interested in taking your vice president of manufacturing, or any of your status quo management team.

## Dell Computers, a Good Example of Lean

The above scenario might be an exaggeration and it may be simplistic, but it isn't all that far fetched. As a case in point, let's look at a real life example, a David against the Goliaths example, which is in full sway as we put down these words. We're speaking of Dell Computers and the tremendous success this company has experienced.

Here's is a startling statistic. In August, 1996, Dell's stock was selling at about $20 a share. One year later, an online price check shows that it was trading at $148.75, an increase of 643.8%.[5]

Dell has done a lot of things right. In only six months the company went from nowhere in cyberspace to being the number one PC retailer on the Web. Sales have been growing 20% each month, and are now more than $1 million a day.[6] One reason is that customers can get precisely the computer they want, outfitted the way they want it, and they can get it fast. From order to delivery typically takes no more than five business days. And, as in our Vanguard Burger example, computers aren't pulled from inventory. Dell doesn't have computers sitting in holding bins or warming ovens. Dell produces only to customer demand. The company has long been manufacturing to fill orders rather than inventory. And Dell just keeps getting better at what it does. Like other lean manufacturers, such as Toyota, it has expanded the concept of just-in-time to its supply chain. The bulk of Dell Computer components are now kept in supermarket-like supply houses within a few minutes of a manufacturing site. It is the responsibility of Dell's suppliers to keep these stocked.[7]

### Kanbans Keep Parts Flowing

Keeping the flow of parts running smoothly requires efficient coordination, the kanban method of inventory and production control. Kanban, a Japanese word that means "sign" or "signal," can be a simple card, often with a bar code, that communicates to the parts supermarket which particular parts will be required to assemble the custom tailored computer just ordered. As kanbans arrive, parts are pulled and sent to the assembly shop floor.

Kanbans also notify Dell's suppliers as stocks are depleted, so that they can automatically replenish the supermarket. You see, it makes sense for Dell's suppliers to employ the same continuous flow to pull method of doing business.

One of the best features of this system for Dell and its shareholders is that Dell doesn't pay for the parts until they leave the supermarket. So, Dell doesn't have money tied up in machines waiting to be sold. It doesn't even have money invested in components waiting to be made into computers.

Consider this. Machines from Compaq and IBM can languish on dealer shelves for two months or more. Yet Dell doesn't start ordering components and assembling a computer until an order is booked. That may not sound like a such a big deal, but it turns out to be. The price of PC parts can fall rapidly in only a few months. By ordering minutes before assembly, Dell's parts are sixty days newer than those in an IBM or Compaq sold at the same time. According to an article in *Business Week,* this can translate into a 6% profit advantage for Dell based on the cost of components alone.

And then there are monitors. In a perfect example of identifying and eliminating muda, Dell stopped accepting deliveries of video displays for its PCs in 1997. Instead, when a machine is ready to be shipped from any of its factories, Dell sends an e-mail message to a shipper, such as United Parcel Service. The shipper pulls a computer monitor from supplier stocks and schedules it to arrive along with the PC. By no longer shipping monitors to Dell first, and then on to buyers, Dell saves about $30 per display in freight costs. Eiji Toyoda himself no doubt would be impressed to see that kind of improvement in efficiency. Figure 1-2 illustrates Dell's business model.

As in the situation just cited, much of what Dell has been able to accomplish has come about by working closely with suppliers in an effort to integrate them into an unbroken supply chain. In the process, Dell reduced the two hundred suppliers it dealt with five years ago to less than fifty today. This, too, is a page from Toyota's lean production manual.

Eliminating waste and improving upon efficiency is not something that true lean producers restrict to the confines of their own facilities. They seek to expand the concept of making value flow to their supply chain by bringing suppliers into the process. And they seek to push the concept of eliminating muda forward all the way to their customers if possible. Dell has done this by eliminating the middleman entirely, and selling direct to the end users of its products via the Web.

### Cash Flow in a Flash

The fact is, Dell is continually trying to squeeze time and waste out of every step in the process of making and selling computers, from the moment an order is taken to collecting the cash. And the company has been highly successful in doing so. For example, Dell converts the average consumer sale to cash in less than 24 hours, by tapping credit cards and electronic payment. By contrast, industry giant Compaq Computer Corporation, which sells primarily through dealers, gets paid in an average of 35 days. Even mail-order rival Gateway 2000 averages 16.4 days.[8]

So let's take one more look at the business Dell has built. The company doesn't have money tied up in machines waiting to be sold because it doesn't make one until an order is booked. Parts aren't shipped until the machines that need them are ordered, and parts aren't purchased until they're shipped. As a result, virtually no funds are tied up in parts. Dell gets paid 24 hours from the time an order is taken, which is about 12 hours *before* the customer takes delivery.

Not a bad cash flow scenario.

# Dell Computer

## Figure 1-2

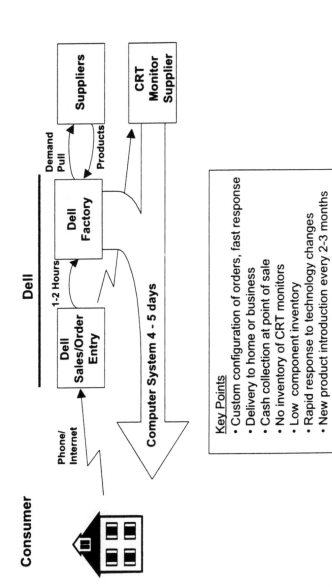

**Consumer**

Phone/Internet

**Dell**

Dell Sales/Order Entry

1-2 Hours

Dell Factory

Demand Pull

Products

**Suppliers**

**CRT Monitor Supplier**

Computer System 4 - 5 days

Key Points
- Custom configuration of orders, fast response
- Delivery to home or business
- Cash collection at point of sale
- No inventory of CRT monitors
- Low component inventory
- Rapid response to technology changes
- New product introduction every 2-3 months

## Rivals Scramble to Catch Up

As you would expect, rivals are trying hard to emulate Dell. PC makers such as IBM, Compaq, and Hewlett-Packard are trying to imitate Dell with their own schemes to slash production time and boost service, but are hampered by their more traditional business model. (Figure 1.3.) IBM, for example, no longer assembles PCs for most of its corporate customers. Instead, computer dealers, such as Micro-Age Inc., do the work. And in June, 1997, Compaq began rolling out its own Internet connection, allowing customers to manage everything from ordering a machine to scheduling software updates online.[9]

Dell is not resting on laurels. Continuous pursuit of perfection is the credo of any true lean enterprise. This is best undertaken by working in a team environment in which each individual understands where the company is going and knows what needs to be done to get there. For this to develop requires communication, training, and the nurturing of esprit d'corps.

## Communication and Training Are Keys

How has Dell gone about this? In one instance, financial teams fanned out to talk with employees about new metrics for running the business, including the need to minimize inventories and increase return on capital. Today, the financial nitty-gritty is deeply ingrained in the staff at Dell. For example, the marketing department calculates the return on investment for each mailing and purchasing managers figure the cost of unsold inventory each day.

"We spent 15 months educating people about return on invested capital, convincing them they could impact our future," said Chief Financial Officer Thomas J. Meredith. This effort is paying off. For every new dollar of capital invested in the first quarter of 1997, Dell shareholders got back $1.54 in profits. This

# Compaq Computer

# Figure 1-3

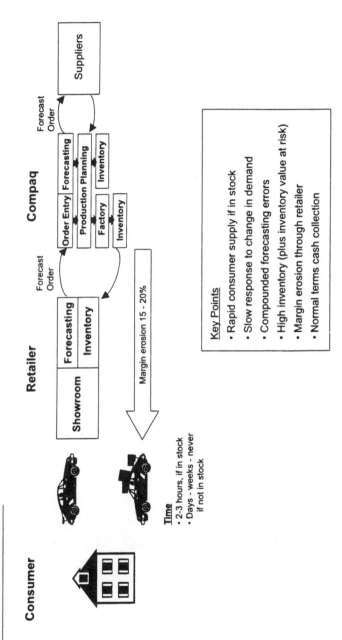

**Consumer**

**Retailer**
| Showroom | Forecasting |
| | Inventory |

Forecast
Order

**Compaq**
| Order Entry | Forecasting |
| Production Planning | |
| Factory | Inventory |
| Inventory | |

Forecast
Order

**Suppliers**

Margin erosion 15 - 20%

<u>Time</u>
- 2-3 hours, if in stock
- Days - weeks - never if not in stock

<u>Key Points</u>
- Rapid consumer supply if in stock
- Slow response to change in demand
- Compounded forecasting errors
- High inventory (plus inventory value at risk)
- Margin erosion through retailer
- Normal terms cash collection

is contrasted with 59 cents for Compaq and 47 cents for IBM.

The company continues searching for ways to improve. Currently, the biggest push is behind selling on the Web where Dell needs a crew of only 30 people to handle more than a million dollars in sales a day. A much larger staff is needed to take the equivalent number of orders via telephone. As a result, Dell plans to make the Web even more attractive by creating custom home pages for its biggest buyers, such as Eastman Chemical, Monsanto, and Wells Fargo. As this was being written, Dell planned to deliver custom e-commerce set-ups to 75 companies within six months. If this goes as planned, the employees of these businesses will be able to order a custom PC from the appropriate e-commerce page and automatically receive the corporate price designated for their company.

## The Dilemma Faced by Established Competitors

It will be difficult for IBM, Compaq and other established computer manufacturers to change the way they do business in order to combat Dell. A host of obstacles stand in the way. These companies have long standing dealer networks and distributors who will not take kindly to the idea of IBM or Compaq selling directly to end users no matter how much waste this may eliminate. But equally formidable will be impediments within the walls of these organizations. It is never easy to change the way a company manufactures, deals with suppliers, handles orders and decision-making, not to mention forecasting, accounting, collections and credit, and the many entrenched support functions that would be affected by a major transformation of the company. Every department, indeed, every function within an established organization, represents somebody's turf, a principality that is likely to be defended.

Middle management's propensity to dig in heels, and what to

do about this, will be discussed later. Unless you are in a start-up situation, it's a hurdle you almost certainly will face. Assuming the role of coach and relinquishing a position as commandant does not come easily. Even the most dedicated and loyal employees may have trouble. We've found workers who don't want to assume new roles even though these new roles potentially offer greater fulfillment and rewards.

## How We Got Where We Are Today

To see how we got here, let's zip over the years since the end of World War II. The war effort required enormous industrial output, and brought people back to work in huge numbers after a long depression. Toward the end, factories in North America were humming. Once peace finally arrived, it didn't take long for them to be converted from tanks and planes to cars, trucks, and refrigerators. And there was plenty of pent up demand to keep the wheels of industry turning. Mass manufacturing was king. People in America felt good about themselves. The mood was optimistic. This time the world truly had been made safe for democracy. People were happy to be alive, to go to school on the G.I. Bill, and to move into a little cottage in a place called Levittown, where baby made three. They shopped at the hardware store down the street, or the five and dime, or the local haberdashery, dress shop, or millinery. If they were really stepping out they traveled downtown to one of the big general department stores. Life was pretty good for a large portion of the population.

Unless one lived through the fifties and takes the time to recollect, it is difficult to comprehend the differences in what existed then and what exists today. The "category killer" stores of today, for example, simply did not exist. Suppose you wanted to buy a refrigerator or a stove? Electric and gas utilities often operated retail outlets that sold these as well as washing machines, toasters and hot water heaters. Variety, choice, widespread information, durability and quality, were not what we have today. Each of the major automobile brands, for example, offered one or two models, the high-priced version of which was differentiated from the low mostly by the amount of chrome that adorned it. These vehicles could be expected to travel 60,000 miles, maybe 100,000 miles, before they wore out. But that hardly mattered. People had just come off of four years of rationing and were happy with what they could get. Besides, back then, folks looked at the world differently. Institutions and government were trusted to do what they were supposed to do, which was to get the job done. Doctors, lawyers and teachers were held in high esteem. Clichés abounded. "What was good for General Motors was good for the country." "You get what you pay for," and you certainly expected to "give an honest day's work in exchange for an honest day's pay." In the evening when you switched on the TV, if you were fortunate enough to have one, you could select from three networks which offered a homogeneous line up of programs such as "I Love Lucy," "Leave it to Beaver," and "The Honeymooners." In this environment of limited product variety and lower quality standards (when contrasted to today's), mass manufacturing continued to serve industry well.

Then came the sixties. The children of the G.I. generation had seen too many episodes of "My Three Sons" to believe any longer that grown ups were infallible. No one older than the age of 30 could be trusted. Behind the gray walls, faceless institutions plotted endlessly to keep people in their place, or so some in our society thought. Nevertheless, whatever their suspicions, business was clicking along, nearing the zenith of the longest peacetime expansion in recorded history. So, with an ever increasing variety of consumer products, the "Me Generation" was born. The battle cry of the day was, "Beat the system."

## The Birth of the Smart Shopper

It wasn't long, in the early seventies, when we saw the emergence of the "Smart Shopper," for whom shopping was viewed as a game that could be won or lost. One of this breed didn't blindly buy at the local hardware or haberdashery. More and more choices in the form of different brands, models and configurations, were out there to choose from. But finding the desired model at the best possible price required effort. One needed to seek out the bargains wherever they could be found. Shopping conquests became the topic of cocktail conversation. The man or woman who died with the most toys had won the game of life. Winning wasn't everything, it was the only thing.

In the early to mid eighties, however, things went downhill. Output could not keep up with demand. Inflation hit double digits. Interest rates went through the roof.

## The Birth of the Couch Potato

People became shell shocked and dispirited. It was common for them to withdraw into "cocoons," according to the parlance of the day. Marketing journals heralded the dawn of the "Couch Potato." Even so, product choices continued to proliferate. The number of different models of cars, for example, was staggering by 1950s standards. From toys, to sports, to household appliances, to hardware, "category killer" stores and warehouse shopping clubs began to spring up in the suburbs everywhere. Nevertheless, for many businesses and individuals it was a time to retrench. Finally, by the end of the decade, inflation was under control, the Berlin Wall had tumbled, the Cold War was finished, and we found ourselves at the dawn of a truly "Global" economy.

## The Arrival of the Possibility Agenda

According to Yankelovich & Partners, the market research firm that's tracked consumer attitudes and trends for well over two decades, as the new millennium is upon us we are witnessing the emergence of what this firm has dubbed the "Possibility Agenda." There is a resurgence of aspiration among the populace and with this a willingness to collaborate. This is accompanied by a new openness to trust that has not been seen in 40 years. Not everyone naively assumes a particular business has his or her best interest at heart, of course, but it is understood that doing what is right and good for the customer usually is smart business. And most are willing to believe that intelligent managers are out there running businesses. People are coming out of the cocoon, if not with enthusiasm, at least with a willingness to give what a business has to offer a try. For marketers, it is a time to pleasantly surprise consumers in order to win their loyalty. The new battle cry that will win the day well may be, "Under promise. Over deliver."

## Shopping Becomes Work

Concurrent with this, the pace of life has become so frenzied that few have time to hunt out bargains or research best buys. Shopping is no longer sport. It is a chore. Work. One strategy is to delegate whatever, whenever possible.

Perhaps this is not surprising. Some huge-scale category killers already have found that bigger is not always better. Once a store has passed a certain size, many consumers decide it may not be worth the effort required to shop there. First, given the size of the parking lot, is the distance from the car to the front door. Once inside, with all that floor space and aisles and aisles of merchandise, it may be difficult to find a particular item. Then, with all that choice, too many decisions may be required once the right section is located. And, when the item is finally in hand, the check out line will probably be too long. As a result, smart retailers are finding ways to make shopping simpler, or at least to bring pleasure back to it. The placement of Starbucks Coffee inside Barnes & Noble Booksellers is one example.

Life also has become extremely complex with the result that a backlash is growing against products viewed as unnecessarily complicated. For example, many have come to realize they don't need a coffee maker that is capable of performing a host of functions they will never need. No doubt engineers are dreaming up the ultimate gizmo somewhere at this very moment. They are likely to learn, to their dismay, that few are willing to pay for the dazzling features that have spilled forth from their imaginations. The time has come to jettison all that is unnecessary.

What does this mean to someone interested in lean enterprise? To be appealing today, technology needs to simplify a consumer's life. High tech for high tech's sake is viewed as too much bother and too expensive. It is not wise to force feed it to customers. Better to offer prospects what they actually need, features that they are glad to pay for. Perhaps the best strategy is to offer the ultimate choice. Let them design and build their own in the manner of Dell Computers. Already, consumers linked to the Internet can "build" virtual cars and trucks with the options they want by going to automakers' Web sites. At this writing, a program called "configurator" is used to locate a dealer that has the consumer's dream vehicle in stock.[10] How long can it be before such programs are used to short circuit dealers all together? Why not send orders for custom designed vehicles directly to the manufacturer for delivery within a few days?

Custom configuring may be some time away in many industries, but shortened new product lead times have become a fact of life. While Dell has been able to accomplish a tremendous advance forward, other industries at least have been able to cut dramatically the time it takes to develop and bring a new design to market. The strategy is to determine what customers want and get it to them as quickly as possible. In the seventies, for example, the process took about four years for the consumer electronics industry. Today, it takes about six months. Reductions of similar magnitude can be seen in many industries, and the pressure is on for more reductions. The thinking is, if you don't obsolete your own products right away, one of your competitors will. Of course, to achieve such speed will require that lean enterprise principles be extended to the marketing function as well as to research and development, and engineering. It probably will mean that you must adopt the Vanguard Burger, continuous flow method of manufacturing. And your suppliers and customers will have to be brought into the loop. None of this will be easy. But if you don't do it, how long will it be before one of your competitors does?

## Value and Your Customer

When all is said and done, what each of us would like when we buy a product is one that performs the tasks we want, works when it is supposed to work, costs as little as possible, and is highly reliable. We do, of course, want service if and when we need it, and we want to have our questions answered promptly and correctly. But we don't care about guarantees or warranties, per se. What we want are *no problems.* Having to return something to be fixed, even at no charge, is a problem. We'd much prefer zero defects at the outset.

Lean enterprise answers all those needs. Moreover, a result of the proliferation of product choices today, and of a global economy, is that it has become very difficult to raise prices. Back in the fifties, sixties, seventies, even into the eighties, if a manufacturer's costs went up, so did his prices. The formula for setting them was "Cost + Profit = Price." No wonder inflation raised its ugly head immediately if the economy overheated. But that's much less likely to happen today. With so much variety to choose from, with so much information on what is available and where to find it, with so much being produced by so many companies all over the world, if the cost of an item goes up, consumers quickly substitute another in its place. This is a major reason why it is difficult to make price increases stick. In many cases, prices actually are headed down. As this is being written, Chrysler has just announced a reduction in the average price of its cars for the coming model year. Ford has said its prices will remain about the same. Toyota certainly isn't going to raise them. What choice does that leave General Motors?

The new equation is "Cost = Price - Profit," meaning that the marketplace will set the price. In other words, target manufacturing costs are driven by the price the market is willing to pay, minus the company's desired profit on an item. In addition, it is becoming increasingly apparent that in today's economy a company must constantly lower its cost to remain competitive. The most effective and sustainable way we know of to do this is through lean transformation. In the future, mass manufacturing simply will not provide a way to compete effectively.

## You Face an Important Choice

If you are like many leaders of businesses today, you face a critical choice. You can be the first in your field to adopt lean enterprise. You can be the first to begin turning out whatever you produce using the Vanguard Burger method. You can be the first to surgically remove every bit of effort and all activities that do not add value for your customer. Or, you can wait until one of your competitors does so first. In the meantime you can hope that nobody in your field makes the move any time soon, knowing that when they do you will find yourself playing catch up. If you wait long enough, you may even find yourself in Frank's shoes, trying to use the old, conventional methods to stay afloat, but all the while sinking deeper into a sea awash in inventory and short term debt.

We are reminded of Charles Darwin's theory of evolution. Though it is still a theory, most scientifically minded folk have come to think of it as fact. Essentially, it says that many variants exist within each animal population. Those which survive to maturity are the ones fortunate enough to have been blessed with certain traits, characteristics, or peculiarities that help them withstand the inevitable vicissitudes of an ecosystem. The others perish early, often before they can reproduce. The result is that the traits conducive to survival are more readily passed on to subsequent generations.

In a stressed environment, one that is undergoing rapid trans-formation, seemingly small differences can translate into big advantages. In the mid-nineteenth century in the English Midlands, for example, when black soot covered just about everything, it was noted that the moths of a particular species had become several shades of gray darker on average than they had been at the turn of the century. The reason was that the trees on which they perched were several shades darker because of the soot. Dark moths were less visible to birds of prey than lighter members of their kin. A shade or two of gray may be a small difference, but it is one which apparently became a matter of life or death for the species.

You probably will agree that the business environment in which we find ourselves today is undergoing rapid change. For one thing, most categories of business now are global. Competition is no longer confined to companies located in your own corner of the world. Perhaps you are not now, but you may soon find yourself fighting for survival. This book offers a way out. And with lean enterprise we are speaking about more than small differences. We are talking about big ones that may enable you to take the lead so that your competitors have to play catch up.

## A Vision of the Lean Producer

The first requirement in making a successful transition to lean is to have a clear vision of what the company will become. You can get there, there is no doubt, but the journey will take time and discipline. All the while you must hold tight to the vision and take consistent actions. To help in this, our goal in this section is to create a picture to hold in your mind.

Let's compare this picture to a work of art. Whether it is a painting, a sculpture, novel, cathedral, or a Broadway musical, true masterpieces are comprised of a host of small details. Little things combine to create a whole that is greater than the sum of individual parts. So, too, is the lean producer. A lean manufacturer is made up of scores of details in the form of procedures, techniques and processes that come together like a symphony to create harmony.

Perhaps more important than any other single element is the attitude, or the culture, of people in the lean organization. We will cover each detail in turn, but first let's examine this.

### The Need for a Championship Mentality

Have you ever been a player, or even the bench warmer, on a championship sports team? Then you know that it is the team that counts, not particular individuals. Indeed, a championship team functions as a single living organism, rather than as a group of separate personalities who have been thrown together. Championship players can recite the play book in their sleep. When game day arrives, every player knows their job. When the whistle blows, each takes appropriate actions that combine like the maneuvers of a precision drill team. A team such as this might be compared to an athlete who has devoted considerable time and energy climbing the Stairmaster, pumping iron, and walking the treadmill. Each cell in such an athlete's body knows its place and the job that it needs to do within the greater whole. It proudly pulls its weight. The dawdlers, fat cells for instance, have long since been expunged.

How does this relate to the lean organization? If you have ever walked into an organization of people who know all the way down who they are and what they are about, you probably experienced the same sense of confidence and esprit d'corps found in the locker room of a championship team. The feeling can be palpable. Individuals who comprise such a group don't define themselves in terms of the role they are playing on any given day. Just as the particular position played does not adequately describe a member of a championship sports team, titles do not define the members of a lean organization. Titles can be changed or be taken away. Lean players and champions are defined from the inside out. Moreover, the boundaries between departments and functions in the lean enterprise are blurred to the point that for all practical purposes they do not exist. Nor does any tolerance for a "not my job" attitude.

A person who has fully bought into the concept of lean enterprise has bought into a mindset that compels the continual pursuit of excellence in order to advance the mission of the organization. The lean player knows a particular job that needs to be done today or next week simply contributes to the greater whole, the bigger task of what the company is about, which is to be the best.

Lean players recognize that mundane tasks are absolutely necessary and must be executed with care and efficiency. They must be carried out professionally because, as in the case of a masterpiece, the smallest tasks combine to create the whole.

One thing is certain. If a task does not, or will not add value to what the company is creating, it should be eliminated. Such a task is muda, and worthy only of contempt. It is unseemly and useless fat.

So even a task that adds value to the end product cannot define the lean organization team member, any more than a position can define a world class soccer player. Just as "goalie" or "wing" does not do justice in describing a World Cup champion, lean organization players cannot be adequately defined as traffic managers, marketing representatives, insertion machine operators, or sales engineers. The lean player and the champion, even though they currently may occupy positions of traffic manager and goalie, are defined by the total organization of which they are a part.

An engineer at a lean company, for example, may be employed in the activity of designing circuit boards. He may even have the title, Chief Engineer, Computer Memory Chip Division. But as a lean player it is unlikely this would be his personal definition of himself. It is more likely he would view himself as a member of a team dedicated to "serving the community by providing products and services of superior quality at a fair price." Likewise, a Wal-Mart employee who has bought into what the company is about will not define himself or herself as a checkout clerk. This individual will find self worth in existing "to provide value to our customers,"[11] just as the Nordstrom sales representative may see his role as offering "service to the customer above all else."[12] If the authors of the best-selling book, *Built to Last*, are correct, a Sony product manager may see herself as being engaged in a worthwhile struggle "to elevate the Japanese culture and national status."[13] And the Walt Disney worker as being part of an effort to "bring happiness to millions."[14]

Workers in a lean enterprise, from the top of the organization to the bottom, know what they stand for because they know what the group they belong to stands for. It is the reason they are in business. This may be the single most important factor in the success of market leaders in general, no matter in what industry they operate. According to the authors of *Built to Last*,[15] the right culture may be more important than superb products, or good ideas, or technological innovation. They theorize that these companies have come to dominate their industries because their employees know that they exist to produce products and services that make useful and important contributions to the lives of customers. Indeed, great products are not what make the organization outstanding. It's the other way around. The organization is what creates great products.

How does a company become an outstanding organization? How does one acquire a winning culture? We will explore techniques for fostering a team atmosphere. But even though shared goals and employee bonding may be important, they are not all that will be required for your organization to become dominant in its field.

Some companies were founded by leaders who themselves had a winning attitude and were able to instill this in subordinates. But for every one of these, there's another that was able to acquire a championship mindset along the way. We suspect that top executives going off to mountain retreats and mulling over core ideologies the company might adopt is not the only way to achieve a championship mentality. Let's consider the Green Bay Packers. This team has an illustrious heritage and has fielded more than its fair share of championship teams. But not always. Between the time of coach Vince Lombardi and the present, the franchise slid downhill pretty far. It was necessary for the team to pull itself out of the dumps. How did it?

Let's say the desire was there. Let's say the team possessed the raw talent and the esprit d'corps. Perhaps, one essential ingredient was missing. How does a team, or a company, come from last place to win the league championship, or to achieve dominant market share, in a few short years?

The answer is that sports teams and businesses both need to master the basics before they can achieve greatness. They must have them down pat, and this takes discipline. Only when they are in top shape, and have the fundamentals honed, will they be able to succeed in a big way.

As was said at the outset of this section, little things combine to create a whole that's greater than the parts. For a football team, this includes blocking, tackling, passing, kicking and ball handling. The lean organization also has fundamentals.

Let's have a look at what they are.

## Fundamentals of the Lean Producer

The transformation typically begins in final assembly with the institution of lean production. It starts with conversion to continuous flow—first one line, then the others. Lean thinking then spreads through the entire organization in order to support lean production, and to purge wasted activity and motion wherever muda is found. Eventually, a lean organization comes to be. But we're getting ahead. First, let's focus on lean production.

Ever visited a metal working shop? Oil-stained floor, right? Now and then you might spot one of those snake-like tubes made of spongy material strategically laid out to soak up a spill. And no wonder, practically everywhere you look, oil can be seen dripping from a machine. Stacks of scrap metal are piled against the walls and in corners. It's noisy with machines whirring and grinders whining, sparks flying everywhere. Metal filings in small heaps huddle here and there. In general, it might be compared to a

# The Lean Production Principles

# Figure 1.4

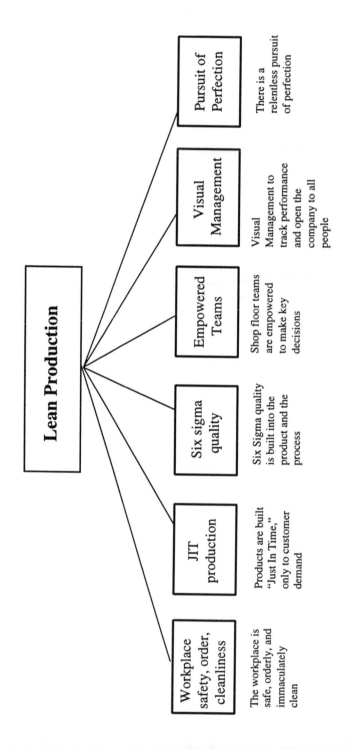

**Lean Production**

| Workplace safety, order, cleanliness | JIT production | Six sigma quality | Empowered Teams | Visual Management | Pursuit of Perfection |
|---|---|---|---|---|---|
| The workplace is safe, orderly, and immaculately clean | Products are built "Just In Time," only to customer demand | Six Sigma quality is built into the product and the process | Shop floor teams are empowered to make key decisions | Visual Management to track performance and open the company to all people | There is a relentless pursuit of perfection |

scene from Dante's *Divine Comedy* depicting hell.

If you conjured up this image, then you didn't visit a lean organization. *The lean organization will be exceptionally safe, neat and clean,* even if it is employed in what is normally considered a messy business. This is so important, and so fundamental, that it heads our list. You see, perhaps above all else stand safety, cleanliness, and order.

Let's quickly touch on the other five characteristics. Then we will return to examine each. (Figure 1.4)

*In the lean organization, products are built just in time (JIT),* and only to customer demand. To do otherwise would be to accumulate inventory, and therefore, potential waste.

*Six sigma quality is designed into the products of the lean producer and built into its manufacturing processes.*

Just what is six sigma quality?

Six sigma quality is a phrase coined by Motorola to represent its drive for the lowest possible failed parts per million.[16] Six sigma represents a mathematical calculation, 99.9996% perfection. This figure equates to 3.4 ppm (failed parts per million), or very close to zero defects.

*Empowered teams represent the fourth characteristic.* Teams of individuals on the shop floor, in the case of a manufacturing operation, or wherever value for customers is being created in a service business, are empowered to make key decisions. When a problem is spotted, the team decides how to fix it. There is no need to call in management.

In an assembly operation, for example, workers are obligated to stop the line if they see a quality defect problem. The line remains shut down until the problem is fixed. This would be unthinkable in most assembly plants. Only the general manager could authorize such an action.

One result of operating through empowered teams is that the

lean enterprise is less hierarchal than traditional businesses. No need exists for layers of supervisors, group supervisors, department heads and so forth leading up a pyramid to the person at the top. A bureaucracy would impede teams and render on-the-spot decision making impossible. Traditional hierarchies usually are not only cumbersome and slow to act, they are costly. Like any and everything that does not add value, in the lean enterprise, the goal is their elimination.

*The fifth characteristic is that visual management is used to track performance* and to give workers' feedback on how they are doing. In other words, management is by sight, not by computer. This often takes the form of scoreboards positioned in easy view of workers. Performance is posted hourly in a column next to preestablished goals. The reasons for variances, plus or minus, are accounted for in a column reserved for "remarks." In this way a team can see where it stands in relation to its output goal for the shift and adjust work accordingly. This also enables indirect personnel to identify obstacles that may be standing in the way of objectives.

Scoreboards are only one example of how information that might remain the domain of a privileged few is brought into the open in a lean producer. The adage that information is power is taken to heart. But rather than being guarded, information is made to flow throughout the organization so that lean players will be empowered to take actions that will improve performance.

*The final fundamental of lean production, and ultimately the lean enterprise, is the relentless pursuit of perfection.* This characteristic supports all others. Players are never satisfied with progress; no matter how far they have come, they don't rest on laurels. The culture ensures a continual and constant search for better ways to do even the smallest tasks. Looking for ways to cut waste, looking for ways to improve quality, looking for ways to cut inventory,

Figure 1.5

## Lean Enterprise Basic Philosophies

- No product is made until the next customer "downstream" requires it

- Quality is designed into the product and process, not inspected in

- Employees are an integral part of the business enterprise, not extensions of machines; employee empowerment is good

- Inventory hides problems and must be eliminated

- There is a relentless commitment to banishing waste and striving for perfection looking for ways to do things better, quicker, faster, easier, becomes ingrained.

But let's not fool ourselves. A substantial difference exists between the declaration of a commitment to continuous pursuit of perfection, and actually doing it. Making it happen requires that a process be in place that forces the reality. This may mean holding daily meetings in which the question is "how can we improve?" It means establishing a mechanism for suggestions and a deadline for responding to them. It means finding and institutionalizing ways to facilitate the free flow of ideas.

So there you have the fundamentals: (1) Safety, order, cleanliness, (2) JIT production, (3) Six sigma quality built in, (4) Empowered teams, (5) Visual management, and (6) The constant pursuit of perfection.

Let's examine each in more detail.

## Safe, Clean, Orderly and Brilliantly Lit

A goal of the lean producer is for the workplace or factory floor to be comparable in cleanliness and organization to an operating room in a top flight medical center or hospital. Like an operating room, the area will be brilliantly lit. As bright as daylight. All surfaces will have a fresh coat of paint, including walls, floors, machines, and counter tops. Every piece of equipment, every tool, every storage bin or cart that belongs in an area should have its own special place, and this place should be indicated by a painted or taped outline of the object. When not in the hands of a worker, these objects should be put away. All potential safety hazards should be eliminated, including wires and extension cords. Everything should meet or exceed government safety standards.

If you do nothing more suggested than take this first step, you will be amazed at the increased efficiency of your organization.

Figure 1.6

## Workplace Safety, Order and Cleanliness

- Safety compliance
    - Very safe, no hazards
    - Rigid adherence to policies
    - Full government compliance

- Lighting, brightness
    - Brightly lit, like daylight
    - Freshly painted ceiling, walls, floors, machines

- Cleanliness
    - No dust or oil on machines,
    - No debris or dirt
    - Floor is clean enough to eat from it

- Orderliness
    - The Toyota 5S program
    - A place for everything and everything in its place

    - All unnecessary items removed from workplace

Quality will also take a jump.

Why?

Imagine the mindset you would have about quality, efficiency, and concern for accuracy, if you worked in a place that was dimly lit, dirty, covered with grease, metal filings in the corners, and stacks of work in progress piled carelessly in the spaces between machines. How much pride would you have in your job if each time you touched something you got grease on your hands or dirt under your fingernails?

Now, suppose all that changed. Suppose you closed your eyes on Dante's inferno and opened them to find the Mayo Clinic?

Slowly, it would dawn on you that you now work in a spotless environment, one that is sparkling clean and brilliantly lit. You might glance down and feel embarrassed because you're improperly dressed. A grease spotted work shirt and jeans with frayed knees are out of place. You resolve to dress differently tomorrow.

You get to work and quickly realize you're able to concentrate much better than before. The lights make it easier to see. It's impossible to be sleepy. Plus, you no longer feel alone, as though your workstation were enclosed within a bubble. The person next door is lit up plain as day. So is everyone down the line. They all look like pros, too, intent on turning out quality work. You feel the same. You're alert and in an upbeat mood.

After a while you discover that you need a screwdriver to make an adjustment. So you hunt for one and are surprised to find the size you wanted right where you'd hoped it would be, in its designated place on a peg board close to your position. It's no longer necessary to waste time and energy sorting through the clutter and looking under piles of rubble. You take a deep breath. You feel good about yourself, and you feel good about the company you work for. The people who run this place must care to have created this environment. They must care about their workers. They must care about their customers, too, because a place this immaculate cannot help but turn out quality goods.

This is a great place to spend the day, and just as important, it's a safe place. A person could have been hurt in that old sweat shop. How many times did you almost have a finger or an arm caught in an unguarded machine, or slip on grease, or trip on a wire? Those things would never happen here.

You get the picture, we're sure. A clean, orderly, brilliantly lit workplace creates a host of advantages, both of a practical nature and of the psychological variety, not the least of which is how workers feel about themselves.

Sometimes the benefits of cleanliness and order are less tangible. For example, both of us ran TRW plants at different times that supplied subassemblies to Japanese automobile companies. Periodically, their management would send in an inspection team. Once, one of the inspectors purposely knocked a part off a dolly, so that it fell several feet to the floor. We quickly realized that the inspector wanted to see what would be done with the component. The fall had put it at risk of being defective.

Fortunately, the worker who spotted the wayward part made the right decision. She put it in the scrap bin. In a sloppy environment, however, this may not have happened.

## JIT Production

In a lean producer, products are built "Just In Time." This means they are built to customer demand, not to sit in inventory waiting to be purchased. You'll recall Frank, the fictional CEO of Vanguard Burger's competitor in the example given earlier. Vanguard had an advantage over Frank's firm because Vanguard was able to give customers precisely what they wanted when they wanted it. Frank was persuaded by his Vice President of

Manufacturing to try to compete by increasing inventory. This seemed a logical way to offer a wide variety, and no wait.

Frank's manufacturing VP was addicted to batch and queue. But finished-goods inventory waiting to be sold, and work-in-progress inventory piled up in batches waiting for the next step of production, is viewed as unnecessary by proponents of lean production. Instead of accumulating either, products are made to flow from the start of production all the way into customers' hands without stopping.

If your business currently employs batch and queue, the VP's addiction will be easy to understand. Perhaps you have high speed machines that perform certain operations. It seems impractical to slow them down in order to slip them into a single piece flow operation. Maybe some of these high speed machines require that dies be changed in order to convert their use from one function to another. These die changes may take hours. Once a machine is set up, it makes sense to get serious use out of it since it would be impractical to switch the machine back and forth during a single day, or perhaps even during a given week, in order to perform functions on short runs. It appears to make more sense to let it run awhile and build a backlog of inventory.

But there's another side to the story. Suppose one of your competitors, just as Frank's did, adopts continuous flow to customer demand? As long as you stay with batch and queue, you'll have only one way to compete. You'll have to increase inventory in order to supply what your customers want when they want it. Like Frank's company, you'll end up cranking out whatever you make in an ever increasing range of varieties. At the very least this will convert into inventory a lot of what used to be liquid assets, and you may have to arrange more credit. So factor in the cost of money tied up as a result of batch and queue in whatever financial calculations you decide to make. You also need to add the direct and indirect costs of the larger facility needed to house the inventory, and the administrative costs of managing it.

Next, think about this. You have a good forecasting system, right? But how often has it been dead on? We suspect not very. The ancient Greek philosopher, Heraclius, reportedly said, "Nothing endures but change."[17] Our experience suggests that he was right. Customer tastes change. New technology comes along. The market shifts. Suddenly, your forecast is as relevant as last week's stock market report.

We're reminded of Osborne Computers, a company you've probably forgotten about unless you happened to have been interested in computers, or were a follower of hot stocks in the early 1980s. Osborne was one of the shining stars of the newly developing personal computer market. The company went from $10 million in sales at the end of 1981 to $100 million in just 18 months. Adam Osborne, the company's founder, said this about what had led to his success, "I found a truck-size hole in the industry, and I plugged it."

The Osborne machine was the first "portable" business computer in that it weighed only 24 pounds (11 kg), was small enough to fit under an airline seat, came loaded with software, and was fairly powerful. Osborne focused all its efforts on this machine. No end could be seen to potential growth in what was presumed to be insatiable demand. In the process, Osborne piled up inventory.

You've probably guessed what happened. Competitors caught up with Osborne in features and technology. Kapro and Compaq entered the market with low-priced machines with as much, if not more, bundled software. But the biggest competition came from a formerly sleeping giant. IBM's personal computer, introduced in late 1981, quickly became the industry standard. Osborne was slow in reacting to and adopting IBM's technology, and equally slow in developing a clone. No doubt this had to do with all the inventory Osborne had to unload. Meanwhile, scores of other computer companies jumped to produce IBM-compatibles. Hardly a year after coming to market, the formerly popular Osborne was obsolete. Even a fire sale of the magnitude Frank staged to unload all those piled up burgers couldn't move them. Osborne was forced into bankruptcy.[18]

Being stuck with outdated merchandise is one of the deadly perils of inventory. Another is that inventory hides problems. Let's say, for example, that you crank up one of those high speed machines in order to stamp a part, or drill a hole, or to form a piece or component. Since it takes a while to get the die changed, you want to make the best of the time and effort you've invested. So you let that baby run, and fill a few bins. These sit for a couple of weeks while inventory on hand is used up. Each bin holds thousands of parts.

The day finally arrives when existing batches run out. A new bin full of parts is pushed into place to feed the line.

Lo and behold, there's a problem. The hole, or the threads, or the curve—or whatever that high speed machine was responsible for—is just a little off, enough out of place that the piece doesn't fit as precisely as it should. You try another piece. It fits a little better. You keep trying. Some fit reasonably well, others not at all.

You step back to survey the situation. You've got three bins filled up from that run. Is every single part slightly off, some more than others? Is there a way to find out? Work backward till you find good ones? Spot check earlier bins?

You try checking parts from early in the run. They're the same—slightly out of whack, some more than others. What are you going to do? If you discard the whole lot, not only will you lose all the money invested in time and materials, you'll lose the time it will take to reset that machine and run what will be needed. You were counting on using these. The whole line will have to be shut down if you have to stop now to run a new batch.

Chances are you'll decide to make do, even though the parts do not fit perfectly. What choice do you have? This will sacrifice quality, and you know it. Some of the widgets you're turning out today are going to come back tomorrow to haunt you. But you've got orders to fill. If you don't move quickly you could shut down production at customers' factories. The choice seems clear. You can get them angry now, or perhaps only slightly irritated later.

Even though batch and queue may seem to make sense on the surface (in this case to use high speed machines efficiently), the situation described is just one example of why continuous flow is better, and consistently results in higher quality products. If the high speed machine could be changed more quickly to make different parts, or replaced with one that performed at a pace that allowed it to be inserted into the assembly line, an adjustment that remedied the problem could have been made the minute a defective part was produced. So, continuous flow to customer pull insures the elimination of work-in-progress inventory that cannot or should not be used. This is in addition to ensuring the elimination of finished goods inventory which cannot be unloaded because of shifts in customer preferences, or because of product obsolescence.

We recognize that for producers that rely on batch and queue, the prospect of converting to continuous flow can be daunting. Not only may a particular machine not perform at a speed that will allow it to be inserted into a line, the need for die changes may be an issue. If a line is run to fill orders (i.e. is run strictly to customer pull), short runs may be commonplace. Once an order for burgers with no onions is filled, the line may have to be converted to make burgers with double onions. What happens if it takes hours to change a set up?

Our experience has been, however, that these impediments can be overcome. In some cases, a different machine, often one that is slower and less expensive, can be found to replace the high-speed model. Or a high-speed model can be slowed down, or perhaps it can be used to feed two or three parallel lines. Dies, or the machines that use them, can be modified so that changes can be made quickly. In a Brazilian plant we converted, 8 hours originally were required to change one of the dies. Workers were able to make modifications that brought this to under two minutes, and this was accomplished with little capital investment.

The key to continuous flow manufacturing is what is known as takt time by lean producers. "Takt" is a German word for musical meter. In lean production, it is the rate of sales in the marketplace, the drum beat of consumption. This is the beat to which to adjust the pace of your manufacturing operation. The goal is to have raw materials, or parts and components from your suppliers, enter one door and flow with hardly a pause as they are assembled into finished goods. These in turn should move out another door, onto the loading dock and into trucks that deliver them to customers.

It may be helpful to imagine your suppliers as tributaries that flow into a river (your assembly operation). The tributaries and the river flow at the speed of sales, your takt time, the pace you want those formerly high speed machines to run. This is the pace you want your assembly operators to work. As you convert to continuous flow, you will probably identify logjams and rapids that need to be balanced. You will be able to speed up passage through the jams, perhaps by adding workers to clear them, and slow the pace in areas requiring less time, perhaps by adding more tasks to be performed by workers there, so that the line moves at a constant speed from one end to the other. Our experience has been that balancing a line can always be achieved.

In the ideal environment, virtually no inventory exists that isn't on its way somewhere. Traffic is directed by kanbans that ensure that an assembly operation doesn't run out of the components it needs. But let's be realistic. Even with an ingeniously devised kanban system, getting rid of inventory can cause operations people to lose sleep. If a machine that makes a particular part goes down and there's no back up inventory, an entire plant could be brought to a halt. So, the total elimination of inventory is a goal to work toward as continuous flow is introduced and the bugs are worked out. You should not expect it to happen the first day. You also might have to keep some inventory of finished goods on hand, for example, to meet peaks in demand that cannot be fully accommodated by continuous flow, due to plant capacity limits. In addition, some inventory of parts and components may be required because suppliers are halfway around the world. Some suppliers also may require that orders be placed well in advance because they still operate in the batch mode.

But don't allow yourself to be lulled into complacency. Think of inventory as a drug. If you are addicted, it is an addiction you must overcome. There are always going to be pushers who will try to keep you dependent. The goal should be to reduce the number of vendors in these categories to an absolute minimum. They should be exceptions that are eliminated as quickly as possible.

Why are we so hard on inventory? So what if a whole batch of components doesn't quite fit? What's the big deal about the possibility of a few product failures?

In the household appliance business, for example, a high number of field service calls not only can be costly, it can be the kiss of death. Most consumers simply will not buy an appliance brand they've had trouble with in the past. This is becoming the case in almost every industry. More and more often, people expect products to work the first time and to keep on working. As we wrote earlier, according to the marketing research firm of

Yankelovich & Partners, to succeed nowadays it makes sense to pleasantly surprise customers with products that are better performers than they may have thought.[19] Quality expectations have become extremely high.

Marketers will tell you how expensive it can be to persuade prospective customers to try a product. Once you have one, it makes sense to hold on. Defective parts can nullify invaluable goodwill. They should not be tolerated just because they come from a batch that someone feels needs to be used up for one reason or other.

Potential defects aren't the only problem. Inventory can hide big opportunities for productivity gains, which may have to do with machine downtime, for example, that can be traced to inattention to preventative maintenance, or perhaps to abnormally lengthy setups. You see, in traditional enterprises a good deal of time often is required to convert a machine from one function to another. This is accepted because production runs typically are long (which creates inventory). For the lean producer, however, changeover must be rapid because items are produced only to demand, meaning that runs often are short. Later, we will discuss in more detail the need for "single minute change of dies," or SMED. In addition, total productive maintenance (TPM) is an issue we'll discuss. The equipment used by a lean producer must run like a Swiss watch because downtime is extremely costly, and more often than not outweighs the expense of keeping machinery in top condition.

Inventory also can hide personnel problems, such as a need for training, or high employee absenteeism. Inventory can hide logjams that need to be cleared, perhaps due to paperwork or product inspections. So, eliminating inventory not only frees up space and capital, it forces an organization to improve the way it works. Once these improvements are made, quality will increase.

Productivity will increase. Major benefits almost always are realized—some predictable, others not.

## Six Sigma Quality

Toyota's plant in Kentucky has about ten slots at the end of the line for cars that need rework. Thousands of vehicles are turned out every day. Yet, if this small number of slots ever becomes full, the production line is stopped so that whatever problem has developed can be found and corrected. This is in contrast to automakers that employ traditional mass production. Most have much larger rework areas that are routinely full of cars. They don't wonder what's wrong. Rework is expected and accepted. These mass producers often proudly point to the large number of "quality inspectors" in white coats they employ. These inspectors actually are engaged in correcting what could and should have been done right the first time around.

Lean producers adhere to the principle that quality should be built in, not inspected in. This starts by having quality designed into a product. Parts are designed so that they fit only one way—the right way. If a process ensures quality, inspection will no longer be required. This is what every lean operation is working toward—a process that ensures flawless products.

It helps to have products designed in the same location where they are built so that the designers are a short walk from the people who will make them. Interaction between design and manufacturing, as well as between other disciplines, should be a requirement. Design teams should meet on a regular basis, perhaps once a week, or even once a day, when a product has reached an intense stage of development. The team should be comprised of the lead design engineer, and at least one representative each from quality assurance, marketing, manufacturing, and purchasing. Plans and alternatives should be discussed at each stage of development. Members of the group critique the design from the point of view of their particular discipline so that potential problems can be identified. Solutions should be offered at subsequent meetings. In this way, bugs will be worked out rather than designed in. Problems that marketing could have foretold if someone had consulted them, for example, indeed are foretold, and eliminated. Glitches in the hand off between design and manufacturing that once appeared inevitable are dealt with before they ever occur.

## Empowered Teams

Empowered teams represent another characteristic of the lean enterprise. For those who prefer a top-down hierarchy, this way of running things does not sit well. In the lean enterprise, however, the role of leaders and supervisors is to motivate, coach, train, and facilitate the work of those adding value, rather than to tell them what to do.

In the case of a manufacturing operation, workers on the shop floor are organized into teams that make decisions or recommendations ranging from ways to improve the process, to who will work overtime, or who should replace an absent worker. When someone is selected by a team for a job, subtle peer pressure invariably ensures that the job will get done.

When a problem is spotted, the team decides how to fix it. Having taken responsibility, the action will likely be made to work, or a better way quickly will be found.

A team is responsible for the performance evaluations of individual members. This ensures that loyalty is directed toward the team.

Each member should be trained to perform all the tasks that may be required by anyone in the group. As a result, team members become interchangeable and can cover for one another or "flex" by taking on additional tasks during slow periods.

Operating through empowered teams means that the lean organization is less hierarchal than traditional businesses. In one plant we transformed to lean, five layers of management were between general manager and shop floor worker when we began. The plant employed about four hundred workers, not a particularly large number, yet reporting to the general manager on the manufacturing side was a head of operations, followed by the head of production, the head of the shop, a layer of supervisors, and a cadre of group leaders. (Each group leader was responsible for a cell of shop floor workers.) This was in contrast to one of the most efficient and productive plants we've worked with which employed more than a thousand workers and had only two management levels. The first plant was changed to look like the second.

## Visual Management

We've all seen managers who guarded information. They may even have kept it under lock and key. After all, information is power. We imagine their line of thinking must go something like this: *If I have it and you don't, that makes me more powerful than you. If I'm more powerful, that makes me superior, doesn't it?*

If employees don't know how the company is doing, if they don't even know how they are doing, how can they be expected to improve?

This is one reason that lean management makes sure everyone in the enterprise knows the size of the company, the sales, and key financial indicators. But it is not the only reason. You'll recall that a sense of belonging, an esprit d'corps, is part of what enables an organization to get ahead and stay ahead of the competition. It's pretty difficult to be proud of what you are, and how you are doing, if you don't know what you are and how you are doing.

Readily available information, information that can be had for the asking, is not all that we are talking about here. We mean making sure people know what's happening, day by day, hour by hour. People should start each day with a brief meeting to review the prior day's performance and to establish goals for the day ahead. Information about how the day is going should be posted as frequently as every hour. In this way, management is by sight, not by computer. Clearly visual charts track through-put of work cells, quality performance, cost and delivery performance, corrective maintenance and machine performance, as well as the training status of individuals, and other team measurements.

The lean factory is a "visual" factory. We've mentioned production line scoreboards that keep an assembly team appraised of hourly production. All around the factory, walls will show charts, graphs and displays that are frequently updated to keep everyone informed about such things as output compared to goals, sales and profit year to date, quality levels, inventory turns, training schedules and the progress made by individuals who are in training. The list of items will reflect what's important for a particular business and group of people.

Instructions for performing procedures are displayed where they are needed, and there are pictorials employing drawings, diagrams, and schematics, rather than written words, which may not be as easily understood.

Kanbans (cards, signs or other means of conveying information) are used to identify arriving inventory and are sent along with empty containers to signal the stock room or a supplier that the time has come to replenish an item. Kanbans accompany products sent to customers, who eventually will return them to signal a reorder. It should be possible to judge a production cell's performance from a quick look at its information board.

In short, information in the lean enterprise is in the open for all to see and use, rather than buried in a computer or locked in a manager's desk.

## Pursuit of Perfection

You probably have noticed a theme inherent in the vision we have attempted to present. It is the final characteristic, an anti-waste mentality or mindset that brings about a constant striving for improvement. Muda, the Japanese word for waste, is the enemy. Expunging muda is a goal that unites lean team players throughout a company. They understand that the organization exists primarily to provide value to its customers. To succeed and excel, they must think of a service or product from the customer's point of view. More likely than not, customers want a product that performs the desired functions, at the lowest possible cost, with no service problems. In order to achieve this, it is helpful to envision the product at each step as it moves the entire distance from concept though production and into the customer's hands. As this is done, it should be determined which activities add value and which do not. All activities that do not add value should be eliminated.

Some wasteful activities may take place outside your organization. Perhaps your suppliers are duplicating efforts, or the distribution process includes unnecessary steps. This is waste, and your goal is its elimination.

A procedure should be in place for suggestions by workers and staff, and a time limit should exist for action to be taken by those in authority. In the most efficient and successful operations with which we've been associated, shop floor teams and leaders meet for ten minutes every single day, so that ideas for improvement can be presented and discussed. In these same plants, if a particular customer is experiencing a quality problem, the operators who make the product are sent to talk with the customer in order to understand firsthand what is at issue, and to discuss how the problem can be resolved. When a worker comes back from such a visit, team members listen carefully because the message has the impact of a peer who has just returned from the front. Workers put on their thinking caps and the problem is quickly solved.

## The Lean Producer Versus the Lean Enterprise

What we have done to this point is our best to paint a picture of a lean producer. But continuous flow production and the other components of lean manufacturing which have been set forth do not fully constitute a lean enterprise. Other functional areas of the business need to have similar programs based on lean concepts. Lean thinking and techniques must be used throughout the organization. This means a flat hierarchy functioning through empowered teams. It means the walls between departments have come down. Wherever it may exist, waste must be banished. Value-added activities must be made to flow in an uninterrupted pattern. Areas of the business such as sales, human resources, product engineering, and process engineering need to mesh. They must work in concert to create value for customers. Indeed, relationships need to be built with suppliers with the same goal in mind. Supplier support and proximity are important facets of what has made Dell Computers so successful, for example. Through supplier supermarkets, Dell has managed to integrate the supply chain into its continuous flow to customer pull operation.

So stay tuned. Part III will be devoted to a discussion of expanding lean practices throughout the organization, and into the supply chain.

Now you see the strategic advantages of a lean enterprise, and have a clear vision. What will it take to make the transformation?

# Leadership is the Essential Component

Strong, committed leadership will be absolutely essential. The vision, and the strength of will to make it a reality, must be present in the man or woman at the top, and in each and every lean change agent throughout the organization. Our goal in this section is to explain why you should not attempt a transformation without committed leadership, and to provide tips for selecting leaders who will not disappoint in this regard.

### The Original Lean Enterprise, Toyota

Two days a month, every month, more than 50 people from all over travel to a sprawling factory complex in Georgetown, Kentucky. They come to have a close look at how Toyota makes cars. The tour lasts five hours and includes an extensive question and answer session. Nothing in Toyota's plant is off limits. No questions are taboo. Toyota doesn't charge a nickel.

Factory tours are nothing new, but this one is so popular that it's booked months in advance. The audience is chock full of competitors. Ford executives and engineers. Chrysler. General Motors. Doesn't someone at Toyota worry that these folks might steal a secret or two?

From our experience working with Toyota, we can assure you the answer is no. A genuine desire appears to exist to promulgate what they believe to be a superior management system. Besides, there's little reason for Toyota management to be concerned. By the time anyone does copy them, if they are even able, Toyota will be well ahead of where they are now because of Toyota's culture of continuous improvement.

There's something else that may give Toyota comfort as well. Even if a competitor knows how Toyota does it, even if they understand from top to bottom, actually doing it, actually putting into practice what's there for the world to see is something most companies, automotive or otherwise, will find difficult to do. People can see and hear Toyota's ideas, and believe that they are good, but the ideas are worthless unless someone with the authority to do so puts them to work. In other words, easy to say, and hard to do.

Even Toyota has some difficulty making its own approach work in factories it builds in countries other than Japan. According to one source, while its U.S. plants are the most efficient in North America, they still require 30% to 50% more time to assemble a car than their counterparts in Japan.[20]

Why? The system requires that people operate in a way that is not customary in most societies. Toyota has spent 50 years in Japan developing a supplier base that works as a virtual extension of its production facilities. The average Toyota supplier in Japan is just 59 miles away and makes 8 JIT deliveries a day. Toyota cannot stroll into a country and immediately have that kind of support. Consider General Motors. The average supplier is 427 miles from a plant and makes two deliveries a day.[21]

### Is Lean Enterprise the Fad of the Month?

There are several reasons a lean transformation may not be easy. Some problems will be simple to overcome. Others won't. Perhaps a few top managers, or the board of directors of your firm resist converting to lean because they don't understand its strategic value. They may see lean as the fad of the month—likely to waste time and money while at the same time causing disruption. There can be no denying that management techniques promising utopia come and go. So, their initial reaction may be to stick to the knitting. "We've done all right running the business the way we have, Charlie. As my mentor back at Old Time Enchilada used to say, if it ain't broke, don't fix it."

Enlightenment should not be difficult to achieve. Ask them to read Part I of this book, or prepare and give a short presentation about *lean enterprise as a strategic weapon*. Watch the gleam form in their eyes as they see how your company can leap out in front of the competition by offering customers choice, quality, fast delivery and attractive prices, while simultaneously cash is generated and the risk of being stuck with outdated merchandise is eliminated. All this, and increases in productivity. Boards of directors and top management are usually the easiest constituency to bring around. Once they realize the potential for increases in the value of stock as Wall Street, or The City, is dazzled by increased earnings, why would they be against it?

## Why Lean Enterprise Won't Happen Everywhere

Another reason for not making a successful transformation may be lack of specific knowledge concerning how to go about it. We're hoping to help reduce that problem. We'll do our best to bring to life the process by giving real life examples of what has worked for us and what hasn't.

Once you know what steps to take and when to take them, who can possibly stand in your way? Just about everyone in middle management, that's who. Stop and think about a lean enterprise. Continuous flow won't work if everything doesn't come together and function like clockwork. Consequently, virtually everything is geared toward supporting the shop floor and the people who work there. This means that the entire organization must redirect its focus. If a machine isn't working correctly, maintenance is expected to fix it immediately. If a part doesn't fit as it should, design engineers are expected to correct the situation post haste. Line operators don't stop to get things. Materials and components are brought to them. If an operator thinks of a better way to do something, process engineers are expected to listen and

## Figure 1.7

### Some Obstacles to Lean Enterprise

- *Top management lacks strategic understanding of Lean Enterprise*

- *Lack of specific Lean Enterprise skills, knowledge*

- *Culture, ego, organizational inertia*

- *Management reluctance to empower people*

- *Fear of change, loss of organizational power*

- *"Not invented here" syndrome*

- *Internal systems and hurdles, specifically --*

    *-- MRPII Systems*

    *-- Inflexible Accounting methods*

    *-- Severely disjointed plant operations*

respond. Supervisors don't tell workers what to do. Empowered teams take on responsibility. The people who where once supervisors are now coaches, team leaders, and cheerleaders. If a worker sees a quality problem on the line, he or she is expected to pull the andon cord and stop production. It's no longer only the general manager who has this authority.

You've heard of a book called *Up the Organization?* Well, we could have called this one *Upside Down the Organization.* Or perhaps *Invert the Organization* might be better. Either way, turning a company upside down is what happens when a transformation to lean is successful. A lean enterprise operates on the knowledge that the rubber meets the road in manufacturing and assembly. With this in mind, it's no longer people in offices with windows and executive suites who are at the top of the heap. All those former bosses now exist to support what was before viewed as the underbelly of the organization, the low rung of the ladder. As a result, the lean enterprise is a company that has been turned on its head.

Most of the former bosses aren't going to go along with this willingly, so you might as well brace yourself for an inevitable backlash. We've seen it happen time and again, almost as soon as the transformation is underway. Middle management, from process engineers, to design engineers, to purchasing and inventory, to floor supervisors, to you name it, are wittingly or unwittingly likely to torpedo what's underway.

Why? Do you know anyone in your organization, or in any other organization, who would willingly give up the status and turf he has gained thus far in his career?

Let's say you've decided to go lean. You map the process. You involve the workers. You tell them how things are going to work. A new day is dawning. They'll be empowered. They'll be making decisions. If they have a suggestion, you want to hear it because

Figure 1.8

## Differences in Business Cultures

### Traditional

- Orders are dictated down the organization; responsibilities reside mostly at higher levels.
- Personnel are frustrated because of limited involvement. "They don't listen to us!"
- Limited communications about the company's goals and performance.
- Limited personal or professional satisfaction.
- Boundaries between functions. Inefficiencies prevail.

### Lean Enterprise

- Decisions are made at lower levels.
- Personnel involved, committed and participating. Proud to belong.
- Continuous pursuit of perfection.
- Extensive communications about company's goals and performance.
- Work provides personal and professional satisfaction.
- No boundaries between functions.

no one knows their jobs better than they. They do them 8 hours a day, every day of the year. Naturally, they're ready with a ton of suggestions. Good ones, too, after years of pent up needs, wants, and frustrations.

You listen. This by itself causes euphoria.

You sort the good suggestions from the bellyaching to find that there are one heck of a lot of good suggestions. You wonder why no one listened before. Together, you and they figure out the best way to lay out the line.

You're working together now. A spirit of teamwork has taken hold. The workers become more enthusiastic. They're bending over backward to make the transformation work. Scrap is down. Defects are down. Output is up.

You move machines around. Eliminate batches. You flow the lines. Balance them. Productivity zooms. Workers are humming and smiling. Throughput jumps 20, 30, maybe even 40%.

Get ready. The backlash may happen right away. Maybe some time will pass. A few days. A week. Maybe you'll even have time to convert another line or two. Inevitably, however, you will run into problems. Not necessarily a backlash. Not yet. We're speaking of problems that middle managers can use as "evidence" that the transformation isn't working. Machines will break down, for example, bringing everything to a halt. Maybe they'll keep on breaking. Inventory will start piling up here. Bottlenecks will occur. The line will go down. Perhaps, it will keep going down. As quickly as a problem occurs and is resolved, another takes it place.

What's going to happen? Keep your eyes wide open. If the backlash hasn't happened, it will now. You'll see it in middle management personnel's body language and demeanor. Arms folded across their chests, teeth gritted. Supervisors will say, "This isn't working." Process engineers will chime in, "I told you our equipment wasn't up to this. It wasn't made for it." Maintenance will say, "We can't drop everything every time a machine goes down." The people whose turf has been tread upon are going to find more reasons than you can possibly dream of for going back to the old way of doing things.

Think. If all these people really believed in what was going on, they'd come to see the occurrence of problems as inevitable. They'd view them as opportunities to work out the bugs, the chance to practice continuous improvement. But if your situation holds true, your managers are going to see them as reasons to return to the old way. We've seen, for example, companies that are held hostage to forecasting or accounting procedures that are incompatible with lean.

"We can't do it this way," your comptroller might say, "we need to measure individual productivity. If you flow the line, everyone will be turning out the same amount. How are we going to administer our incentive program?"

The answer, of course, is to change the incentive program. Make it a group incentive plan, instead.

"But what about the union?" will be the next question. "They aren't going to sit still for this."

We're willing to bet that the union will cooperate if they are informed about what is going on. The union wants what's good for its members, and we're almost certain that union members will tell their leader that lean production is good.

Do not be mistaken. Unwillingness to change is what you are encountering. Unwillingness to change and the guarding, or retaking, of turf. In our experience, this can only be overcome in one way, and that's through the willpower of a strong leader. The leader must say, "Wait a minute. I see what's happening here. You like the way things used to be. You don't want to change. I understand where you're coming from. But I'm afraid you're going to have to get over wishing things would return to status quo. It isn't going to happen. So get with the program, or get on your way out the door."

If the leader doesn't take a stand, perhaps hoping that people will come around, he or she runs the risk of losing what has been gained, allowing the transformation to go down the drain. Workers quickly will lose enthusiasm, and quickly will become cynical if conditions revert to what they have always been. They will come to believe you were crying "wolf" if it again takes 3 weeks to get a new drill bit. Do not allow this to happen.

You must be willing to stay firm, and allow your company to see clearly that you're serious, or you should not begin. Trying to convince everyone a transformation to lean is a good idea will not make it happen. The transformation must start with you.

## Transforming from Manager to Coach

Many successful managers have spent their entire careers being the ones who came up with the good ideas, and then pushing them through. They also aren't used to or comfortable with others having them. They may feel that the successes in productivity the company has scored in its transformation reflect poorly on them. Suppose, for example, you are the head of process engineering. Suppose a lean enterprise change agent comes in and works directly with line operators. In a week or two, the line is laid out differently. Work is redistributed. Productivity jumps 30%. Until now, process engineers had been responsible for deciding how the line was laid out and distributing work among operators. And productivity jumps 30%. It appears they were not doing their jobs. How do you suppose they are going to react?

Unless they are much bigger than most people, they are going to be angry. Or, perhaps they will be genuinely incredulous. Either way, they are going to say that the gains cannot be sustained. This prophecy will come to pass if you allow them to undermine the progress made. We have actually seen situations where industrial engineers have dismantled a line that had just been improved in productivity by 30% in order to revert to the old methods.

What these engineers need to realize is that lean is a new way of working. It isn't something that was taught when they were in school. They also need to realize that more good ideas will be generated if the process is opened to everyone. This includes the line operators. A good idea is a good idea, no matter where it comes from or who has it. What's important is that a good idea is put to use. Think about the power inherent in everyone putting their mind to coming up with one. The opportunity for improvement would be immense. And in the lean enterprise, that's what management is for—making sure good ideas are put into practice.

Team play, decision making down the line, and thinking first of the customer are what make the Toyota Production System (TPS) the envy of automakers on every continent. Team play is what lean enterprise is about. As a result, a thorough reorientation of everyone in your company may be required. Managers must let go. They simply will no longer be in a position to give orders. They have to become coaches. Workers must take responsibility. Operators have to be willing to stop a line if quality is at risk. Everyone must work together. A shift must take place from an authoritarian climate to one that is participative. What's good for the whole must take precedence over what may be viewed as good for an individual.

How is this climate created? How is one-upmanship overcome? How can a company set aside "us and them" thinking?

The process must begin with education. People must know that a big change will be necessary, that this change may go against basic human nature (to guard personal turf), but that anything less will not be tolerated. A strong leader, a benevolent dictator, will be required because people simply aren't going to change out of the goodness in their hearts. It is a "lean enterprise paradox" that the leader of a successful transformation must possess two qualities that seem to be in opposition. He or she must be dictatorial, and at the same time, empowering.

The transformation must proceed along a clearly defined route toward a clearly defined vision. This cannot be negotiable. The route and the vision must be clear. Yet, the leader must empower teams, must give them the leeway and the authority necessary to make the transformation happen.

Indeed, it must be made clear that everyone will have to adopt a new way of relating to others in the workplace. For this to be accepted, for this transformation to work, it may be helpful to know that the required change is a natural step in the growth and evolution of people and businesses. Scientists and philosophers may disagree on many things, but there's one issue on which they're in accord. All of nature is interdependent. Everything, from people to quarks to galaxies to black holes, are seamlessly intertwined. We become increasingly aware of this as we mature. Eventually, we come to understand that a life of abundance is impossible if we aren't willing to rely on others, or reciprocate by ensuring others can rely on us.

The same principle is true of lean enterprise. All individuals and businesses are interdependent throughout the value chain. A weak link can shut down the whole. Companies or the individuals that ignore this should be aware that they do so at their own peril.

## Be Prepared for "Concrete Heads"

It is a fact that some people will have difficulty with all this. A small percentage of workers and managers will simply be unable or unwilling to change behavior that has become as much a part of them as their hairstyle or the clothes they wear. Each year at Lean Summits arranged by Dr. James P. Womack and Professor Daniel T. Jones,[22] we have the opportunity to talk with others who have undergone lean transformation. Almost without exception, "concrete heads" are viewed as the most serious obstacles to progress. These are managers or workers who are extremely uncomfortable with the new way of working. Their behavior ranges from talking the talk but *not* walking the walk, to taking willful action that undermines the transformation.

One executive told a story about his vice president of manufacturing that bears repeating. After much planning and many conversations with individuals throughout the organization, the day came for our acquaintance to brief his entire management team on details of the coming transformation. Marketing, research and development, purchasing, engineering, sales, and operations managers from throughout the company were gathered in a hotel ballroom. The CEO stepped forward to make his remarks. The VP of manufacturing and other top executives flanked him on the dais. The intended message of their presence was that everyone in senior management stood behind the move. But it soon became apparent this wasn't so. The VP of manufacturing had never argued about going lean, nor had he voiced any concerns. But he let the entire room know he opposed the plan by rolling his eyes and shaking his head as the CEO outlined certain actions. His body language may have been unconscious, but he clearly let everyone know where he stood. As a result, confidence was severely undermined.

A number of managers at these summits have told us that if they had it to do over, one thing they definitely would do is get rid of concrete heads quicker. This is something to keep in mind, but you also should know that it is possible to turn some concrete heads around. In more than one instance, an individual who at the outset was a naysayer was transformed into a proponent of lean. In other cases, the horse was led to water, but could not be forced to drink.

Here's an example of an operations manager who was brought into a badly deteriorated situation. Productivity was in the basement when he arrived. Expenses were through the roof. Production was so backed up that customers were very unhappy. The assembly operation, which normally ran two ten hour shifts four days a week was now running 24 hours a day for 5, 6, and sometimes 7 days. Overtime along with time and half pay was so common-place that most workers no longer were interested in taking more. Needless to say, the unit was operating in the red.

The new manager saw immediately that the organization lacked discipline, so he moved quickly to establish authority. He issued a directive that not a decision was to be made, no overtime was to be authorized, and not a purchase order was to be written without his approval. Noting that the assembly operation was in disarray, he hired a cadre of supervisors whose job it was to clamp down and keep a tight rein. He met with them daily and issued strict orders. He got tough, fired troublemakers, and refused to put up with foolishness. He wore a scowl. Fear spread, and with it came order.

Soon, the situation was no longer out of control. Within 3 or 4 months it had stabilized. The backlog had been cut to a manageable level. The work week was down to 4 days, where it belonged. Profitability was now slightly into the black.

This manager deserved a pat on the back, correct?

Yes, and he got it. Given the state of affairs when he'd arrived, his actions may have been necessary. He did not go about change the way we would have. His techniques were old school, to say the very least. Nevertheless, he was able to achieve a respectable degree of success.

We arrived on the scene and evaluated the situation. It was our view that having stabilized the organization and established discipline, the time had come to begin the transformation to lean. Layers of management needed to be reduced. Decision making would have to be pushed down to line managers and assembly teams. The authoritarian approach, if it ever really had been necessary, had served its purpose. We believed what was needed was for teamwork and esprit d'corps to be fostered and allowed to work.

How do you suppose the manager felt about this? As you might expect, his expression did not resemble one of those little round smiley faces. Nevertheless, he said he'd do his best. He allowed a lean enterprise change agent into the plant, and this change agent began working with one of the production line cells. Within a couple of weeks this line had made enormous productivity gains.

It wasn't long before we heard via the grapevine, however, that the executive in question had directed his subordinates to "play along" with us and with the change agent. They were to *pretend* to be working toward the lean transformation—but only while we and our agent were present. Then it would be back to business as usual.

Needless to say, we were not pleased. But we could understand why he felt as he did. He'd turned around a bad situation in a short time. Even so, the line that had been transformed to continuous flow was producing at a remarkable level. Couldn't he see this? We went over the figures with him.

He stubbornly acknowledged the gain.

Something in our gut told us his was a hopeless cause, but we decided to give him the benefit of the doubt and with it, another chance. We applauded him for the turnaround, and for doing what he felt he must to make it happen. We told him we were convinced that his plant was in position to become a showcase, but only he could make it happen. He now had a model to follow, the line that already had been converted. What was required would be to expand the transformation to the other assembly lines, and eventually throughout the organization into every area and department.

Then we told him about rumors he was sandbagging lean transformation. We explained that the decision to go lean had been made at the highest level. It was going to happen; no exceptions would be allowed. His plant would have to be brought into the fold. We laid out the metrics which had been established as goals. If specified progress was not made toward them within 6 months, we'd be forced to find someone who would make it happen.

He agreed to accept the challenge.

What took place, however, was a thorough disappointment. The story is sad but true. The lean change agent went on to his next assignment. In his absence, the steps toward lean which had been taken were dismantled. The transformed production line was returned to its old way of working, and to its old level of productivity. Shop floor workers became disheartened and cynical. The plant still was only marginally profitable six months after the ultimatum had been given. No progress toward goals had been made. The manager was given his walking papers, and a new manager was brought in.

If we had that one to do over, the scenario you have just read would not have played out the same way. We'd have seen the signs well ahead, and that manager never would have been put in charge. We'll tell you those signs shortly, but first, here's an example of a different general manager. His plant had recently been acquired in a merger, and it was already a fairly efficient operation. When the manager first saw our presentation on lean enterprise, we'd have guessed from his body language that we were going to have trouble making him a convert. He sat with his arms folded across his chest, a frown on his face. Now and then his eyes appeared to roll back in his head.

This man saw the lean enterprise presentation a second time when it was given to his boss and the boss's immediate subordinates. The boss was unabashed in his enthusiasm for lean. Apparently, this enthusiasm did not go unnoticed.

And this same man saw the presentation a third time when it was shown to key managers at his plant after our lean transformation change agent showed up at his door. By then, the manager's demeanor had changed. The change agent received a warm welcome. Machines were moved and several batch processes eliminated. In no time, throughput picked up.

Workers were given more authority. Kaizen teams brainstormed ways to do things better. New procedures were implemented.

In a short time, the plant's productivity, including both direct and indirect labor, had improved by 40%. Output was way up with the same number of workers. Payroll was down significantly because overtime no longer was required.

Then the inevitable backlash occurred. It happened when maintenance personnel became over extended and could not keep up with the demands that were being put on them. (In a lean production facility, equipment must work when it's supposed to. If a machine breaks down, it will bring an entire line to a stop. So it has to be fixed immediately.) Middle managers used this and every other pretense that could be dreamed up as evidence that lean transformation wasn't working, and should not be continued.

The general manager called his staff together. He explained that the company was not turning back. He was committed to lean transformation. Nothing would or could stop progress. He realized, of course, that adjustments would have to be made. More maintenance personnel would be hired. Or better yet, personnel would be transferred from areas now overstaffed, and trained in maintenance. The manager went on to say that this was probably not the only hurdle the plant would have to clear on its way to lean. Other difficulties surely would arise. They, too, would be met and overcome. Anyone holding out hope that the company would revert to the old way of working would be better off to let go of that illusion, and get with the program. If they didn't like the new way, and weren't willing to help make it take hold, they should start now looking for another job.

In this way, the uprising was put down. The crisis passed. The transformation continued. Today, that plant is well on its way to becoming a model lean enterprise.

What was the difference between these two managers? Both were intelligent, and had been successful in their careers. Both appeared to have had good reasons to want to make lean work. Why did one refuse to accept the concept, while the other eventually embraced it as his own? Could the second manager have been more highly motivated than the first? His plant had recently changed ownership as the result of a merger. He had new owners, new bosses who obviously were enthusiastic believers in lean. The manager was in his fifties. Finding a new job at his age might not have been easy. Yet, an ultimatum was never issued, and from the outcome, not required.

The first manager also was in his fifties. It was obvious that his superiors, too, believed enthusiastically in lean enterprise. He was actually told he would have to find a new job if he didn't make the transition happen. Yet it appears he didn't even try.

Why?

Might he have felt more secure because of his recent successes?

He had indeed turned around a bad situation. He may have believed that the goals placed before him could be met using the old, traditional way of working.

We suspect this was indeed the case.

In contrast, the other manager saw the potential offered by lean. Again, we must ask ourselves, why?

Over the years, we have observed that some managers have a tendency to embrace lean, and that others simply do not. This tendency, or lack thereof, appears to be part of an individual's personality makeup. It has nothing to do with age. You can get an indication of whether or not people possess the tendency by talking to them. Ask them to describe themselves. For example, if they were forced to choose between "practical," or "innovative," which adjective would they select? The people who see themselves as innovators are likely to be better bets in going lean.

Keep talking to your candidate. An individual who will have a difficult time going lean is one who will describe himself as firmly grounded in reality. He will say he wants facts. He remembers facts. He believes in experience, and he knows what works and what doesn't work through experience. On the other hand, the individual who has potential to become a lean change agent is likely to focus on the future and the possibilities it holds. The "possible" is always in front, pulling on the imagination like a magnet. The future holds an attraction that the past and the actual do not.

A difference can be seen in the way the two managers in our recent examples process information. The potential foot dragger, or concrete head can never have enough data. True to their preference for experience over innovation, they want facts. Lots of them. Once they have collected a pile, they will want more. It may seem that they can never have enough before they will even consider changing anything.

On the other hand, the potential change agent does not continue gathering information ad nauseum. He wants and values data to be sure. But once he has enough to see a pattern, or to support a hunch or theory, he will take action based on the pattern or coherence that he sees. For him, the information simply "hangs together" to support a course of action. He may continue gathering data after he himself is already convinced, but this is to prove his point to potential naysayers.

Although the change agent is tolerant of established procedures, he will abandon any that can be shown to be counter-productive or indifferent to the goals they seemingly serve. Not so with concrete heads. They are so in tune with established, time-honored institutions and ways of doing things that they simply cannot understand those who wish to abandon or change those institutions.

We have met and worked with many managers who fall into one category or the other just described. Under normal circumstances, individuals who fall on the concrete-head side can be effective administrators, even though it simply isn't part of their makeup to be visionary leaders. They can be quite valuable to an organization, if they are placed in positions where the objective is to maintain status quo. Unfortunately, transformation to lean is not a normal circumstance. It requires someone at the helm who is willing to step out front and take risks. It requires an individual who is constantly on the lookout for new and better ways of doing things, someone who is stimulated by possibilities, and is constantly motivated by a restless feeling that there are better and more efficient ways. This is your change agent, and he or she needs to be put in charge.

Depending on the organization, however, individuals with what it takes to be change agents may not stick out to the point of being obvious candidates. In younger days he may have raised his

Figure 1.9

## Word and Idea Preferences

Concrete heads:

- Past
- Experience
- Time-tested
- Traditional
- Facts
- Sensible
- No nonsense
- Perspiration
- Actual
- Down-to-earth

Lean change agents:

- Future
- Innovation
- Speculative
- Imaginative
- Hunches
- Possibilities
- Ingenuity
- Inspiration
- Intuition
- Theoretical

head out of the foxhole and been shot at enough times that he learned to keep a low profile. The end result is, he may be cautious about revealing his forward-looking tendencies. After a while, like most people, he may have become slightly stuck in the trap of conventionality. It may take some coaxing to get him to venture onto the battlefield again.

To illustrate, let's return for a moment to the two managers who were just described above. Manager number two, who became an agent of change, did not at first openly accept lean concepts. But, as you recall, he saw the presentation on lean enterprise three times. This, combined with enthusiasm on the part of his superiors, was enough to open his mind. He took the ball, and ran with it.

The manager who turned out to be a concrete head also saw the presentation several times. But it simply was not part of his makeup to be an agent of change, even under pressure from his superiors. He was too wedded to tradition. He preferred "proven" ways of operating. He selected the likelihood of having to find another job rather than implement change he could not bring himself to embrace.

We might infer from this that when presented with an approach that isn't their own, even potential change agents may appear to dismiss the approach without much thought. An effort may be needed to get them to open their minds. Repetition may be required. Sitting through a presentation of lean concepts several times, for example, can make the difference. A friend of ours in advertising has spent years and hundreds of thousands of dollars studying the effects of various amounts of exposure to advertising. According to him, the first time a person sees something new, whether it's an ad or anything else, their reaction usually is to categorize what is seen in terms of existing knowledge. Suppose, for example, a person sees a purple cow.

The reaction might be summed up as, "What *is* that? Oh, it's a *cow*, isn't it? Yes. Except, it's a *purple* cow." Once they've got this in a pigeon hole, they feel free to move on.

The second time they see the cow, their reaction is likely to be more personally evaluative. "Ah-ha. There's that purple cow again. Odd. But what does it mean *to me?*"

If they decide that the purple cow has relevance for them, the third and subsequent exposures will reinforce this. They may take action after the second exposure, or many more may be required to push them over the line. Our change agent, for example, got on board after only three exposures.

If a person decides that the purple cow has no relevancew, as in the case of the concrete head, no amount of repetition will be convincing. Subsequent exposures go in one ear and out the other, having no positive effect.[23] That person's mind has been made up. The conclusion is that repetition can be important and helpful in making converts to lean, but only if those potential converts are innovators by nature. They must possess a built in uneasiness about holding to the status quo. They must be future and possibility-oriented.

Let's turn our attention now to the people who aren't the leaders and aren't expected to be, those who may come around eventually, but are not themselves change agents. Suppose everyone in an organization was put on a bell curve. Change agents might be placed on the extreme right, and concrete heads on the extreme left. The group that comprises the big hump in the middle is everyone else. You aren't expecting them to lead the charge, but you do want them to follow. If they don't, the best place for them is out the door.

How much time should you give them?

It's naive to think that people who have been working a certain way all their life are going to embrace lean enterprise without a period of adjustment, even if they may have a few of the requisite characteristics or tendencies. To go lean, they will have to give up an approach they are accustomed to, an approach they have grown fond of and are comfortable with, one that's worked and taken them where they are. It's like saying goodbye to an old friend, and may even be as traumatic as getting divorced.

## The Stages of Adjustment to Change

We're not psychologists, but we've been told that predictable stages are passed through when someone deals with a loss or a change in status quo. Stage One is denial, as in, "There's been a mistake. I'm sure I put a quarter in the parking meter." Yet the parking ticket is right there under the windshield wiper.

It happens all the time, so be prepared. When you tell a manager about the changes needed to transform to lean, he or she may think you aren't being serious. He or she may believe that by ignoring you, you'll forget about it and life will go on as always. "This isn't happening," he or she may say. "If I just nod my head and smile, this will blow over."

If you aren't totally committed, this approach may work. But let's say you stick to your guns. Next will be anger.

"The boss can't mean it. Not after all I've accomplished. Well, this time I'm not going to do it. I'm valuable to this organization. I can't be forced to do this."

You stick to your guns. Bargaining follows. "Okay, I understand, now. But, some customers aren't going to like it. You'll have to agree, it's better not to rock the boat. This continuous flow to customer demand, for example—spreading out deliveries instead of taking a month's supply at once—we can't force them. We'll have to make some exceptions."

Once more, you hold your ground. The fourth stage is depression. You may notice a change in his or her body language.

Slumped shoulders. Dark circles under the eyes. It's as though the individual were saying, "I've tried to tell them, and they won't listen. There's only one thing left to do, and that's to go out into the parking lot and eat worms."

Once he or she has reached this stage, you're practically home free. Give moral support as it is needed. It is a team effort and everyone is valuable. "Chin up, and iet's get on with it." Chances are he or she will move on to the fifth and last stage, which is acceptance. Then you've got yourself a lean player.

Forewarned is forearmed. In your briefings prior to the start of transformation, it will be helpful to tell your managers and workers that it's normal for them to pass through the stages we've described, so that they'll understand what's happening to them. This will not circumvent the process of adjustment, but it will help speed it along.

### Personal Transformation will be Required

You will also want to explain that to successfully transform the environment, to become a true lean enterprise, people in the organization must transform as well. Seeing ourselves and others in a new light is the first step. It's something that we must do, not only in our jobs, but personally. Rather than thinking of ourselves as supervisors or line operators, for example, we must see ourselves as coaches or key players on a team. Rather than regarding others as co-workers or subordinates, we must come to view them as fellow team members.

How does one go about a personal transformation? How does one reprogram oneself? Surely, some will think this is impossible. "I was born this way. I can't be somebody I'm not," will be their position. They're wrong, of course. Anyone can change, whether losing a hundred pounds is the goal, or changing how we relate to others.

In his book, *The Seven Habits of Highly Effective People,*[24] Stephen Covey writes about a realization that altered his life. He was wandering among stacks of books in a college library when he came across one that drew his interest. He opened it, and was so moved by what he read that he reread the paragraph many times. It contained the simple idea that a gap exists between stimulus and response, and that the key to our growth and happiness is how we use this gap. We have the power to choose in that fraction of a second. If we see a photograph of a creamy chocolate sundae, we can choose to order and eat it, or we can decide on raspberry sherbet. Or no dessert at all. If we see a fellow worker who happened to be our subordinate yesterday and who appears to be having difficulty with a particular task, we can direct another worker who also happened to be our subordinate yesterday to help. Or we can be the one to help.

Richard Carlson, the author of *Don't Sweat the Small Stuff . . . and It's All Small Stuff,* picks up on the same idea.[25] His advice is always to take a breath before speaking or taking action. If you adopt this, you'll rid yourself of the habit of reacting. You'll begin taking a considered approach, and taking a considered approach can lead to all sorts of good things such as better relationships with friends, family, and co-workers. It can lead to a slimmer waistline. It can even lead to your transformation from commandant to coach.

Another way is to become what some have called a "silent observer" of yourself. The idea is to move your point of view out of your head, and place it on your shoulder or the ceiling. Then watch yourself go about your business. Once you start keeping an eye out, you may see things that aren't helping you get where you want to go. From here, it's a short step to self transformation. Especially if you take that breath before reacting.

## You're Still Going to Have Concrete Heads

Let's say you communicate all this to your workers and managers. Let's say you develop a seminar or training program and have them take part in it. You still need to be prepared to deal with some who simply are not going to make the transformation. More must exist than a willingness to change. It takes desire, and some won't have it. Their personal identities may be too closely associated with their jobs. The jailer sees himself as a jailer. He can't picture himself as one of the inmates, even if he gets to be a key player on the inmate soccer team. The commandant views himself as the commandant. Being commandant is what gives him his sense of self worth. He simply will not allow himself to become the coach of the boys in the gulag.

Decide in advance how you're going to handle these cases. Stay alert to the stages, and set a time limit for them to take place. If a worker is not making progress, if it looks as though he or she will never be a team player, perhaps there's a solitary job that still will need doing after the transformation. Move him or her into that job quickly. Don't allow a few bad apples to spoil the bunch. The transformation to lean is worth the effort, but never easy. It will be impossible if you allow even a few people to stand in the way.

## Let People Know What to Expect

When the time comes to begin the transformation to lean, management will need to get people together and let them know what is going to happen, and what they can expect. A meeting or series of meetings should be held in which plans, objectives, strategies, and the reasons for the transformation are communicated. The purpose of the meetings is to create a vision for the immediate future, a road map that will eliminate as much uncertainty as possible during what is sure to be an uncertain time in the company. People should understand why the decision to go lean has been made, that it is essential to remaining competitive, and that it is the only sure way to achieve the company's goals. And they need to know how the transformation will affect them. For example, their value as workers will be enhanced. They will receive cross training that will make them multi skilled. They can expect satisfaction with their jobs to increase. They will become empowered. A cleaner, safer working environment will be created. They can expect the company to grow and expand, which will create opportunities, some of which may flow to them.

What marketing research people call "early adaptors" and we have called "change agents" will pass through the stages so quickly that you may not see it happen. But it will take time for others, and a few never will. In our experience, concrete heads will number about the same as early adaptors. But slow pokes need to come around or be out the door for the transformation to take on a life of its own. How much time you allow is a judgment call.

Be firm. Give them time, but not too much.

Δ Δ Δ

## Key points and Highlights

In Part I, we have attempted to give an understanding of why lean enterprise is the ultimate strategic weapon. Based on our experience, within a short period (months, not years) it is possible to see dramatic improvements in your company's quality, productivity, delivery performance and asset utilization. The space required for manufacturing may be reduced by as much as 50 percent. Additionally, while it will require time and effort, inventory may be cut from its current level to two or three days. Returns because of defects will be virtually eliminated. Moreover, lean enterprise is much more than a formula for operational excellence. It can enable you to give customers what they want, when they want it, while cutting your costs and lowering your defect rate.

How? By setting up your plant like Vanguard Burger, or in other words, by employing continuous flow production to meet demand created by customer wants and needs. By systematically identifying and eliminating waste. By extending lean enterprise principles to all areas of your business including marketing, engineering, and research and development in order to shorten new product lead times. By bringing your suppliers and your customers into the loop so that value-added activities are made to flow from the beginning to the end of the production and distribution chain. And finally, by never letting up. No matter how much you are able to achieve, continuously and relentlessly pursue further improvement.

None of this will be easy. But your competitors aren't likely to copy you, at least not immediately. They will find thousands of reasons why lean enterprise is not a good idea for them. But to compete they will have to increase inventory. And at the very least, this will deplete their cash. In the long run, it will be virtually impossible for them to stay competitive using conventional

94

methods.

If you are like many business leaders today, you face a golden opportunity. You can be the first in your field to undergo lean transformation. You can be the first to employ continuous flow to customer pull. You can be the first to trim every bit of waste and all activities that do not add value. You can be the first to deliver precisely what your customers want when they want it with products that are virtually defect free. Unless you are starting a business from scratch, this will not be easy. Nevertheless, we are certain that the benefits to you, your employees, customers, and shareholders, will be well worth the effort.

Perhaps the most notable ingredient of a lean organization is a winning attitude. Some companies were founded by leaders who themselves had a winning attitude, but for every one of these, there's another that was able to acquire the mindset along the way. The first step toward mastery is to master the basics. Here they are:

*The lean producer will be exceptionally neat, safe, and clean,* even if it is employed in what is normally considered a messy business. This is so important and so fundamental that it heads our list.

*In the lean producer, products are built just in time (JIT),* and only to customer demand. To do otherwise would be to accumulate inventory, and therefore, potential waste.

*Six sigma quality is designed into the products of the lean producer and built into its manufacturing process.*

*Empowered teams make decisions.* There's no need for layers proceeding up a pyramid to the person at the top. Bureaucracy gets in the way of progress.

*Visual management is used to track performance and to give workers feedback.* Information flows freely. Lean members are empowered to take actions that will improve performance.

*The final fundamental of the lean enterprise is the relentless pursuit of perfection.* The primary goal is to provide value. This pursuit is ensured by procedures that institutionalize the search.

Lean transformation will not occur, however, without strong leadership because going lean turns a traditional business on its head. The other functions of the business become support for what may have been thought of as the low rung of the ladder. As a result, a backlash by middle management is inevitable. This must be put down quickly.

In choosing lean change agents, look for individuals who consider themselves to be innovators. They are comfortable acting on the pattern they perceive in a situation. Concrete heads can never have enough data, no matter how compelling. They are guardians of the status quo.

# PART II

## The Lean Factory

W e've found that there's a logical sequence for the implementation of lean. With this road map, and a thorough knowledge of the six fundamentals previewed in Part I, you will have what you need to begin. Let's quickly lay out the road map. Then we will proceed with a detailed discussion.

As already written, the lean transformation usually begins on the factory floor. The objective is to make production flow precisely to the takt time of customers' needs. We usually begin in final assembly. It is best to pick a specific area (e.g. a product line) that can be transformed within a few weeks, so that the "lean team" can gain experience and confidence.

## A Brief Overview of the Key Steps

First, map the final assembly process for the area to be transformed. (An excellent book on mapping is *Learning to See,* by Mike Rother and John Shook, published by The Lean Enterprise Institute, Brookline, Massachusetts. For more information, see LEI's website, www.lean.org.) Next, clean and organize all areas to be changed, taking care to get rid of all items that are not necessary for the production process. Then install continuous flow. Next install a kanban "pull" scheduling system between the order entry function and final assembly to link production to customer takt time.

Once these steps are complete, it's time to begin working progressively backward in the production process. Use the kanban system to link final assembly to internal and external component supplies. Reduce setup times and batch sizes (especially in stamping, molding, plating, PC board insertion, etc.). Steadily reduce defects in the manufacturing process through root-cause problem solving. The goal is to have perfect parts flowing from your suppliers to your company precisely timed to the takt time of customer demand. During the entire process, employees should be trained in this new method of manufacturing. They should steadily become empowered to control more of the process. While this is proceeding, visual management systems should be installed.

When a production line is complete and is operating reasonably smoothly, it's time to begin again with another "slice" of the factory. The process will be repeated again until the entire factory is complete, and suppliers and customers are fully linked on a pull-scheduling basis. This may take as little as 6 months or as long as a year depending on the size, complexity, and level of vertical integration in a given factory. In Part III, we will travel beyond the shop floor to the entire lean enterprise, but for now, let us stay focused on the factory.

Let us discuss how you can apply the six elements of lean production.

## Workplace Safety, Order and Cleanliness

Most people underestimate the importance of safety, order and cleanliness in the workplace. Our former colleagues at Toyota and Honda will tell you that 25-30% of all quality defects are directly related to this issue. An unsafe, dirty, disorganized factory will generally have poor quality. By contrast, a safe, clean, organized factory will produce much higher quality. There is also an important psychological component here. Shop-floor employees will be much happier and more productive when working in a clean and attractive place. Conversely, people who work in a cave-like atmosphere will behave like cave dwellers— not so happy, not so productive, and generally not quality conscious.

Figure 2.1

## The Toyota 5S System

• Sort (Seiri) - Separate out all the items that are unecessary and eliminate them completely from the workplace

• Straighten (Seiton) - Arrange all essential items so that they are clearly marked and easily accessed ("A place for everything and everything in its place"). Use kanban squares to identify the location for key items in the work area.

• Scrub (Seiso) – Scrub all machines and the work environment to maintain immaculate cleanliness.

• Systematize (Seiketsu) - Make cleaning and organizing a routine practice as part of the work day.

• Sustain (Shitsuke) - Sustain commitment to the previous four steps and provide a constantly impoving process.

Toyota probably has the simplest and best system for workplace safety, order, and cleanliness. They call it the "5S" system, appropriately named after five Japanese words we've listed along with approximate English translations:

## Sort

This step is like cleaning your attic, but is more ruthless. There is no room for sentiment. Before beginning this step, make sure you have a large waste-disposal dumpster. You'll be surprised at how quickly it fills up. Your objective is to get rid of everything that is not absolutely essential to the manufacturing process. Sort items into "Definitely Needed," "Maybe needed," and "Not Needed." Everything that is not needed for this process (or for any other in the factory) goes straight into the dumpster. By the way, make sure you have someone from Accounting who can log the fixed-asset tags of disposed items so that they can be written off the books. Segregate the "Maybe Needed" items off to the side. When you have finished the 5S process, anything left over from Maybe Needed goes into the dumpster (i.e. you didn't need it after all).

A note is warranted here about personal items on the line (e.g. backpacks, handbags): There is no place for them and they in fact can cause safety and quality problems (e.g. straps caught in machinery, items falling into the production process, contamination). The best way to secure personal items is in individual lockers (with locks) that are not on the production line. (They can be immediately adjacent to the work cell if this is more comfortable for the operators.)

## Straighten

Once you have disposed of all non-essential items, the next step is to "straighten" and organize the work areas. Here we are creating "a place for everything and everything in its place."

First of all, the general arrangement of equipment in a work area should be neat and orderly, following the sequence of the production flow. If the layout is a straight line, the equipment should be lined up along the line. If it is a "U" shaped cell, equipment should clearly follow the line of the "U." If we are "5S-ing" a department of machines (e.g. plastic molding or stamping), the machines should be laid out in a logical grid pattern or something that makes it visually easy to see the organization and flow of the workplace.

All cables and hoses for equipment should be transformed from a jumbled tangle of snakes to bundled sets that are organized and neat. It is especially important to make sure that cables do not pose a safety hazard. All items, such as tools, will be organized onto shadow boards where the outline of the tool is visible on the board. This way, when the tool is missing, it is readily apparent. Here again, there is a safety component. We remember looking one time at an automatic insertion machine for electronic components. Some of the tools for adjusting the inserter heads had been placed inside the machine, near the movement of machine's mechanisms—a major safety hazard if the tools were to become lodged in the rapidly moving parts. (Not to mention the damage to a $250,000 machine.) When we asked the operator why the tools were there, the person said it was "more convenient" than storing them outside the machine. Of course, this person also didn't know if all the tools were immediately available when the machine did require adjustment, and (as we found out later) often spent a lot of time (with the machine not operating) searching for the needed tools. We had the individual develop shadow boards for the entire auto insertion area—much to the delight of the entire team.

Kanban squares are also used to organize loose items in a work cell. A kanban square is merely an outline (outside perimeter) of the item that goes in a designated space. The outlines are usually done with removable tape, although they are sometimes done with paint—and the space is labeled, describing what goes in the space. For example, a box of paper towels used for cleaning would have a taped outline marked "paper towels;" other items might include trash bins, lubricating oils or pallet locations for final packing at the end of an assembly line. Obviously, the term kanban square is only loosely descriptive; the outline of the item can be any shape at all (e.g. rectangle, circle, trapezoid) whatever makes sense. For marking large areas (e.g. for finished goods storage or pallets) one of our colleagues suggests using the Tensator belted lane separators that can be seen in the check-in line at an airport.

Flow-thru racks are another important 5S tool. Flow-thru racks are generally used for material handling of components, work in process, and finished goods. They serve the purpose of clearly organizing these materials, clearly labeling their location, and providing critically important first in, first out (FIFO) control. FIFO control is essential to the quality process.

The previous paragraphs are meant to illustrate, and do not provide an exhaustive list of ways to organize the workplace. Again, it is important to keep the objective in mind. The organization of the workplace should follow the flow of the process; it should be free of any safety hazards; there should be "a place for everything and everything in its place." All items should be clearly marked and identified.

## Scrub

This "S" is probably the easiest to describe. Some books and training programs refer to this "S" as "Spic and Span" or "Shine." Both are acceptable and descriptive. We simply prefer to use an action verb.

All equipment, tools, work surfaces, floor areas, etc., should be scrubbed until they are immaculately clean. As a customer, how do you feel when you walk into a dirty factory? Does it give you a feeling of confidence about the quality of the product and the reliability of the supplier? Generally, the answer is no. We had a recent experience in an electronics factory. The first two S's had been done fairly well, but very little had been cleaned. All the equipment and component racks had a thick layer of dust. The floors were not clean. Did this project an image of quality? The customers certainly didn't think so. Conversely, once the areas had been scrubbed, the attitude change of the customers and the employees was dramatic.

The objective should be to make the saying "you can eat off the floor" true. In addition to scrubbing, walls and machines may need a new coat of paint. Windows should be cleaned. Marred or chipped work surfaces should be repaired or recovered.

### Systematize

Once the workplace has been cleaned and organized, it is imperative to keep it that way. In other words, "Systemize" the program. We won't prescribe a set method. Rather, methodology should reflect the culture of the organization. In one Brazilian facility where we worked, an organized and regular review of workplace cleanliness and organization is called the "SOL" program. This stands for Segurança (Safety), Orden (Orderliness), and Limpeça (Cleanliness). SOL is also the Portuguese word for sun. Under the SOL program, cross-functional teams use a standardized checklist on a regular basis to evaluate the company's departments. The teams employ a "lost points" evaluation method whereby points are deducted for infractions. The results of each evaluation are posted for all to see. Training for this program is extensive and extends to all employees in the plant. It is rigorous, thorough, and highly effective. For example, the metal stamping department is immaculately clean. No oil is on the floor. The machines sparkle with cleanliness. All stamping dies are placed in fixed locations for each die in clearly labeled racks near the presses. And, there are potted plants (yes, live green plants) on the floor (in kanban squares, of course). The entire factory is spotless, and a pleasant place to work.

## Sustain

Sustaining refers to making the 5S program a way of life. It differs from "systematizing" in the sense that this refers to setting up a system to maintain the 5S program. "Sustaining," on the other hand, is the continuation of a strict commitment to the entire process. It means that every employee understands the importance of safety, order, and cleanliness, and takes action every day to ensure that high standards are met. Visit a Toyota factory at any time, day or night, and you will see the commitment to the program. A special clean up is never necessary simply because an important visitor is coming. Toyota facilities are always properly maintained.

As an interesting historical note: The 5S program used to be called the 4S system, however, the fifth "S" was added to demonstrate the need for continued discipline in making the other S's a way of life. Our own experience illustrates this. Upon early initiation of 5S programs in our facilities, both of us discovered that it required constant policing. Frequently, last minute clean ups were needed when visitors were coming. It became clear (with some input from Toyota) that our employees did not understand the importance, and therefore were not committed to it. After a new round of in-depth training, specifically on the 5S's, the concept finally was embraced.

Whether you adopt Toyota's program or create your own is

not important. The critical thing is to incorporate the concepts of safety, order, and cleanliness into your lean enterprise program.

### Beyond the 5S's Lighting, Appearance, and Brightness

The best facilities we have seen have not only an excellent 5S program, but are also brightly lit, have flooring that is sealed, tiled, or brightly painted, and have white or light colored ceilings that reflect light. Outside of North America, it is common to have skylights, windows, or other sources of natural light in the factories. When we walk into a facility such as this, it almost takes our breath away. The feeling is always, "Wow."

In summary, to be world class, a business needs to look world class.

## Building Products Only to Customer Demand

In lean production, as you are now well aware, all actions are pulled by customer demand. Production needs to flow to the customers at the rate at which they order the product. For this reason, the conversion generally begins at the place closest to the customer, final assembly, and works outward to the rest of the operation.

### Takt time

Takt is the drumbeat of consumption, the speed at which products are ordered by customers. As mentioned before, the word takt comes from German and means meter, as in musical meter. The goal of a lean producer is to build products at that rate, not faster, not slower.

The customers' takt time is sometimes easy to determine, and is sometimes difficult. One of the authors (Henderson) ran a seat belt company that was a member of the Toyota group. The seat

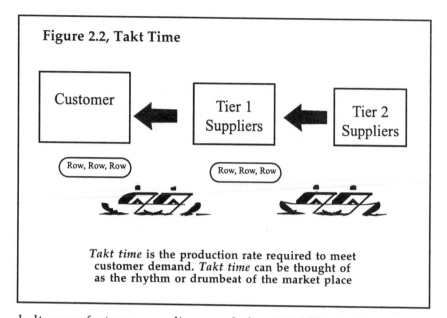

**Figure 2.2, Takt Time**

Customer ← Tier 1 Suppliers ← Tier 2 Suppliers

Row, Row, Row          Row, Row, Row

*Takt time* **is the production rate required to meet**
**customer demand.** *Takt time* **can be thought of**
**as the rhythm or drumbeat of the market place**

belt manufacturer supplies seat belt assemblies to Toyota and other auto companies. Toyota's overall takt time was straightforward. They made approximately 1,000 cars per day, every day. There are five seat belt assemblies per car, two front belts, two rear outer belts, and one rear center (lap) belt. The front belts were made on one assembly cell, the rear outer belts were made on a second cell, and the rear center lap belt was made on a third cell. The buckles that accompanied the seat belts were made on a fifth cell. The customer demand to be produced by the front seat-belt cell was 2,000 per day (two belts per car times the 1,000 cars per day currently being assembled). Two shifts totaling 14.5 hours of production time were available to make the belts. (In calculating production time, don't forget to subtract for ergonomics, i.e. lunch, breaks, clean up, etc.) This meant that takt time was 26.1 seconds. (You can calculate this as follows: 14.5 hours x 60 minutes x 60 seconds = 52,200 available seconds. Divide by the 2000 units demanded to get 26.1.) On this basis, takt time is quite straightforward. It becomes more complicated when we consider that the cell must also produce passenger-side and driver-side versions, each in four color variations. Now we have eight variations to be produced on the same cell. What should be the takt time for each? The answer is that the cell must produce one seat belt assembly every 26 seconds regardless of what configuration is being made. In fact, we did not know more than 24 hours in advance exactly what combination of color mix and front/rear belts would have to be made. The line had to be flexible enough to make any combination with a changeover from one version to the other in less than a minute. (By the way, at Tokai Rika, Toyota's seat belt supplier in Japan, the order lead time was only 4 hours.)

Computation of the takt time for Mazda was more difficult. The seat belt manufacturer supplied only a portion of the seat belt assemblies for Mazda's factory. While Mazda's production line rate was quite steady, the daily orders to the seat belt manufacturer varied significantly depending on Mazda's product mix on any given day. In this case the internal takt time was set by agreement with the customer, i.e. we established a capacity to produce 500 car sets per day. Mazda gave us a 5 day firm shipment schedule (given on a Thursday for the following week's production). Although the delivery volume fluctuated significantly from day to day, the weekly volumes were reasonably constant. The team leader on the final assembly cell set the daily production schedule by taking the next week's requirement divided by five, ensuring that the line was producing approximately a day in advance to ensure 100% on-time delivery.

We once worked with a facility that served a distribution market. As a result, a large number of customers placed orders in quantities as small as one for many different items.

How can takt time be established in such a case?

It is important to understand the concept behind takt, which is to produce an item at the rate the market needs it. Demand on any given day determines the volume to be produced that day. Calculating this number can be accomplished using a spreadsheet program on a PC, and totaling the number of each item needed.

The concept of takt time can be extended to any customer demand situation. For example, Doyle Wilson, president of Doyle Wilson Home Builders in Dallas, decided to make his home building company a lean enterprise. In his computation of takt time, he determined that he was completing 2 homes per day. Therefore, all his internal systems (e.g. architectural plans, construction drawings, cost estimates, and actual construction) were geared to produce homes at this rate. (More on the Doyle Wilson Home Builders story can be found in *Lean Thinking*, by James P. Womack and Daniel T. Jones.)

In a pure service industry, the takt time would be determined by customer demand for the service. In an appliance repair business, it would be the average daily service call rate. In commercial banking, it might be the average daily demand for loans. In this case, all paperwork processes would be set up to meet that requirement.

What about situations where a customer's takt time, based on their ordering patterns, appears to vary enormously (e.g. daily requirements fluctuate 30% or more). We see this in two situations. The first is one in which there is an actual change in demand (as in the case of Mazda above), and the second, is when customer's MRP (A.K.A. "Materials Requirements Planning, or Manufacturing Resource Planning) system drives enormous swings in supplier orders and/or is programmed to order in large batches. In both cases, it is necessary to calculate the average of one or more week's demand. This is easy if you know a customer's actual production line rate. You can then tie your internal production to that line rate and "filter out" the wild fluctuations caused by the customer's MRP system. We'll talk more about this issue under pull scheduling and kanban.

## Kaizen Event

As indicated earlier, you will want to begin by mapping the operation in its current state. You will then develop a new flowchart according to how the process should take place in order to support continuous flow production. Mapping means drawing a picture, or a diagram of the production process. By mapping things as they are, everything that is relevant will be taken into consideration. After mapping has been completed, decide what is being done that adds value, and what does not. A mass manufacturer with disjointed operations typically will have an "as is" map that looks like spaghetti.

The next step is to redesign the process by "flowing" what adds value, and eliminating the rest. Implement the new process and measure what is accomplished. Often, this is called a "kaizen event."

By flowing the process we mean making value-added activities move along without interruption while non value-added activities are eliminated.

Map things as they are. Measure and eliminate what does not add value. Flow the process, measure again, celebrate the success. Then start all over again. Keep working back from final assembly until the whole company is one continuous river of value-added activity.

The same idea can be applied in the service sector. A financial process, engineering process, or anything similar is certainly a candidate, provided the same steps consistently are taken. An advertising agency, an accounting or architectural firm can apply the principle. Each has jobs that flow through the organization.

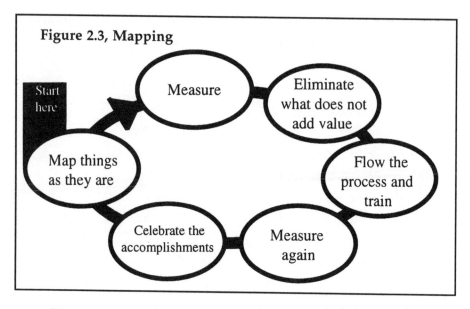

**Figure 2.3, Mapping**

Start here · Measure · Eliminate what does not add value · Flow the process and train · Measure again · Celebrate the accomplishments · Map things as they are

Map the steps from job initiation through development, final layout and copy, client approvals, and whatever steps are required to bring the work into final form. For an architect, this would be blueprints. For an accounting firm, perhaps an audit. For an ad agency, it could be film that's shipped to a magazine or video cassettes to television stations. Whatever the situation, mapping effort will probably reveal that some steps add value and others do not. Eliminate the offenders unless they are absolutely necessary for legal reasons, or because of client dictates. You may find, for example, a client no longer is concerned that forms be filled out in triplicate.

Mapping requires a thorough understanding of the process and all possible variations on it. Consider, for example, a plant that assembles electronic devices. Many different items often can be built on a standard stuffed, printed circuit board because loading different calibrations into a board's memory can create a multitude of variations. Let's say that this is the case with 90% of what a particular plant turns out. Infrequently, however, a need may arise for a non-standard board, say for a device that isn't built often. An order may come along every three months, so the non-standard board may not be kept in inventory. In this case, the board may have to be made from scratch, so assembly begins by placing components in a board, rather than at calibration. If you don't allow for this variation, you're going to develop a big headache the day an order arrives.

It is important to understand precisely what it is that is being mapped. Mapping a manufacturing process usually is more straight forward than mapping a service process. A product can be viewed moving through an assembly process, and determine what is and what is not adding value to the product. But let's consider a service process.

For example, the process followed by an order from the time it is received through shipping and collection. In this case, what we are mapping is "information flow."

What happens when we receive the order? How is it tracked? What kind of approvals are required? How long does the order wait in line? How long is it before the shop is notified that we need to manufacture the product? All this needs to be mapped and measured. Then, we can see what adds value, and what does not. Flow the value-added activities. Eliminate the others. Train everyone. Implement the new process. Measure again.

As you can see, this is what was done for a manufacturing process. The same would be valid for an engineering design process. The approach is applicable to everything we do, not only customer service, but finance, sales, purchasing, engineering—in a nutshell, to every operating process inside a company, regardless of what the company does.

**Figure 2.4**

Batch

Continuous Flow

## Continuous Flow Production

The next step after mapping is to convert the production process from batch to continuous flow. This will involve converting the process map to an actual shop-floor layout, balancing the line on paper, physically converting to the new configuration, and then restarting production.

## Straight lines, U-Shaped, or Other Configurations

We are conscious of an ongoing debate about the best configuration for assembly lines or cells. Some prefer straight lines, others prefer U-shaped cells with operators looking outward from the U, others prefer U-shaped cells with operators facing each others, still others like ellipses. We do not believe there is a right or wrong way, although consistency within a plant will likely promote harmony. Physical space considerations, material flow, and the culture of the people must be taken into account. Here's a word of caution: In very long, straight assembly lines, it is difficult to establish a high degree of teamwork and real-time communication among the operators.

## Balancing the Line on Paper

First, using the new process map, do a rough cut balancing of the line. The objective is to have each operation or group of operations match the takt time of the line (which will match the takt time of the customer demand). The line balancing exercise will determine how operators are assigned to specific machines and operations. For product to flow continuously and without interruption, each operation in the manufacturing process must take about the same length of time. For example, if one operation requires less time than the others, the operator will have idle time. On the other hand, if a product doesn't move through a station as fast as it does downstream, the downstream operations will be starved of product. Measure the time an operation takes and distribute the work in an effort to have each operation take the same amount of time. Make sure to determine the touch time, which is the time that an operator actually spends touching the product. This is important to know. If touch time is longer than machine time, it may make sense to move all or part of an operation to another location. If machine time is longer than touch time, you might give an operator additional responsibilities.

One of the facilities where we worked had a painted steel-based board on which available floor space was diagramed. Cutouts were made of workstations, using magnetic paper. This allowed potential layouts to be easily configured and reconfigured. They could be repositioned until an arrangement was found that produced the best result.

Another method is to use Scotch stick-ons, which allow for easy pick up and re-stick. The team can test configurations until the best potential alternative is found. Note that we say the "best potential alternative." Only by putting one into practice will we know for certain.

We should note as well that it is critical to include some (or all) of the operators when balancing the line. They are the most knowledgeable concerning how the operations actually work.

## Rearranging the Line

Rearranging the line is fun, so why not make it an event. Have the entire line participate. Make a poster board of the new process map so that everyone can see the configuration. You can use the magnetic based board approach mentioned earlier, which will also allow you to make changes as experience demonstrates the need. Include maintenance people or outside contractors to move air lines, reroute cables or install new electrical fixtures. We've seen some cases where the team has actually made a cardboard mock-up of the new line in an attempt to anticipate potential glitches before they happen. It's also important to review the new configuration with the entire team, including initial operator assignments. This is also the time to perform 5S activities for the areas being rearranged.

## Restart the Line

Now restart the line. You will need to make adjustments to the line balance quickly. Inventory will build up in front of locations that need to be speeded up. Places will become apparent where operators have idle time, or where inventory is required so that it can be pulled to keep the line moving. These may need to be slowed. Line balancing often can be achieved by redistributing or combining functions. Some activities might be moved from one station to another. In our experience, there is always a way to balance a line, although several attempts may be required.

## Practical Considerations and Helpful Hints

*Single Piece Flow:* When we speak of continuous flow in

manufacturing, we're referring to what is often called "single piece flow." In its literal interpretation, single piece flow means that there is a maximum of one production piece between each operation. In fact, we've seen some cells where there is literally a single kanban square between each workstation that says "Only One Piece!" At the risk of speaking heresy (as seen by lean production purists), we've found that adhering strictly to a single piece between operations is not always optimal. You may wish to flow more than one piece at a time. For example, suppose each worker on the line spends only 5 or 6 seconds performing her function. What happens if someone sneezes? Suppose he or she drops something and has to pick it up? With only a few seconds between parts, the line will stop and start like cars in a traffic jam. Design the system to keep things moving—which may mean three, four or five pieces between operations in the line. Continuous motion, with as little inventory between stations as possible, is the goal. The right amount will depend on an individual station's touch time. But be careful. If you become lax about inventory, we've found that two or three parts will have a tendency to multiply. If you don't insist on a maximum, say five parts as the absolute top end, eventually you'll end up where you started, with batches between workstations. To avoid this, it is imperative to define the number of allowable parts between each. Use kanban squares, chutes, or other methods to limit the number of parts that can build up. The rules must be clear: If the maximum number of parts is reached, the operator must stop work. This is how line imbalances and bottlenecks become clear.

*Availability of Materials:* The line must have a constant supply of materials in order to maintain continuous flow. In a later section on kanban, we will discuss material handling in more detail. What needs to be remembered is that bringing components, raw materials, and/or subassemblies to the final assembly cell is part of the process, as is the packing and movement of finished goods. In laying out a continuous flow process, material storage locations and replenishment frequencies must be taken into account, and team members must be assigned this task. It is critical that the line does not stop due to the need for materials.

*Changeover Time:* The goal is to change a final assembly cell from one model to another in one takt time. In the case at the seat belt company described earlier, the changeover time was 25 seconds. When changing from a passenger side to a driver side seat belt, for example, the new version was started at the first operation of the cell and each subsequent station changed as the new seat belt arrived at that station. A clothespin was clipped to the first seat belt in the new series to indicate that a changeover was required. The clothes pinned belt traveled around the cell signaling to each operator that this was a new series, and a changeover was required. A similar event occurred when there was a color change. The cell could make any of 8 varieties of belts, each with a 25 second changeover. In another facility, the marker was the product to be made next, painted in a bright color and modified to resemble a locomotive, in this case a small control. The point here is that the change can be signaled by any means that is clear. Operators' creativity can be used to come up with an indicator.

*Dealing with Batch Operations in the Middle of a Continuous Flow:* It is not unusual to come upon a process that has a batch operation in the middle of what you want to convert into continuous flow. For example, some epoxy resins used for potting of printed circuit boards may require a curing oven. Or perhaps a washing process is needed in the middle of a machining operation. The short-term way to deal with these batch processes is to build the batch operation into the process using kanban squares to accumulate the proper batch size in front of the process, and another kanban square at the end of the process to receive the batch-processed parts.

In this manner, you are inserting a batch-processing delay into the continuous flow process. This is not optimal, but much better than a pure batch process. As quickly as possible you will want to convert the batch process to a continuous flow, using "right-sized" equipment, i.e. a piece of equipment that is sized properly for a smaller operation.

Here are two examples. One of our factory teams took several batch-machining operations and put them into a continuous flow cell. The huge batch parts washer was replaced with PVC pipe, water lines, buckets, and drains. The team created a series of water chutes and buckets that did the cleaning. In this way, the team reduced throughput time from several days to a few minutes. Total investment was about $400, and all items were purchased from the local hardware store.

In another case, a large batch heat-treating oven (a true dinosaur) was replaced with a countertop oven with a continuous flow conveyor. We've seen many such cases where the teams have come up with creative solutions, often requiring little investment.

*Cross Training of Operators:* Cross training of the operators on the assembly line is crucial to the success of a lean producer, as we will see in the next two sections on "Maintaining Continuous Flow" and "Flexing the Line." Cross training means that every team member on the line is trained to do all the jobs on the line. This requires that all operators be multi skilled, which provides a benefit that may not be obvious until put into practice. Operators can rotate jobs regularly. Not only will they stay fresh, the quality of output will stay high because there will be less boredom with mundane or repetitive activities. There should also be fewer injuries from repetitive strain.

Frequency of rotation, by the way, should be left up to the

workers. They may prefer to shift positions every hour, every few hours, or once a day. Of course, people need to be trained in all operations, but this can be organized and coordinated by the group itself, and for the most part, done on the job. Each individual might spend a few minutes a day learning a new task, or they might spend several hours. The most proficient at a task, the old timers, become teachers who pass their skills to others. This in itself becomes a source of job satisfaction. Besides, becoming multi skilled has several benefits that can accrue to the

**Figure 2.5**

| Production Multi-Skill Chart | | | | | | | | | |
|---|---|---|---|---|---|---|---|---|---|
| Department: Assembly | | | | | | Date: 03/11/97 | | | |
| | 3way RIG RPI 151-80 | Valve Machine RPI 151-84 | Button Sub Assy to Body RPI 11-82 | Shank Assy Test RPI 151-86 | Shank To Body Assy RPI 151-87 | Packing RPI 151-93 | Rework | | |
| Drapeza, Merie | ★ | | ★ | | ★ | ★ | ★ | | |
| Ferris, Julie | | ★ | ★ | ★ | ★ | | | | |
| Micallef, Lilly | | ★ | ★ | ★ | ★ | ★ | | | |
| Santos, Nimfa | ★ | ★ | ★ | ★ | | ★ | ★ | | |
| Wong, Nancy | ★ | ★ | | ★ | | ★ | | | |

workers being trained. They feel better about themselves and are more valuable to you. We've found they usually are enthusiastic about learning new jobs and skills. Try developing a training progress chart and mount it on a wall where all can see it. List every worker and have a column for each skill. Check off the skills as the worker has mastered them. As the number of checks grows, so will a worker's pride and spirit of professionalism.

*Flexing the Line:* If the assembly line is designed to produce 120 units per hour, and the customer demand falls to 75 per hour, what do you do? The traditional answer is to build inventory because you don't want to have bad efficiency numbers. However, as in the case of Osborne Computers related in Part I, this can lead to waste (or ruin) because customers may stop buying the model. In a lean environment, (assuming the demand slowdown will continue for more than a week or so), you slow the rate of production to match customer demand. This action will usually take the form of using the same equipment, but with fewer operators. You might decide to deploy seven instead of ten, and have these seven "flex" to cover what would be more workstations in a full-capacity situation. Or, in some instances, neighbors can flex and take over the job while the worker is gone. As an organization becomes more adept at being lean, the teams will usually do line balance studies for varying levels of output and assign team members to specific operations accordingly.

Due to equipment and process considerations, a finite number of throughput volumes exist that allow for a balanced line. It is important to understand this to be prepared for situations such as an operator being absent for the day with no replacement available. It may be impossible to balance the line with one less, so resist the temptation to proceed on this basis. (See Figure 4.7) To avoid timing being thrown off, and the attendant disruption, the next level down that permits a balanced operation should be determined. It is common for a chart to be developed that shows the line volumes that support a balanced operation, and the number of operators required for each.

What do you do with the excess operators when you have "flexed down?" They support other teams, undergo training, or work on an ongoing quality problem or improvement opportunity. They are not sent home, but rather continue to contribute to the entire team and the organization.

*Maintaining Continuous Flow:* Traditionally run operations allow for 15% or more downtime for personal needs such as going to the bathroom or making a phone call. When there are large batches of parts between operators, taking a 5 or 10 minute individual break does not cause a problem (other than lost efficiency). But in the lean production facility, the objective is to maintain continuous flow production. If someone must leave the line for any reason, another team member (sometimes the team leader) must cover for them.

**Figure 2.6**

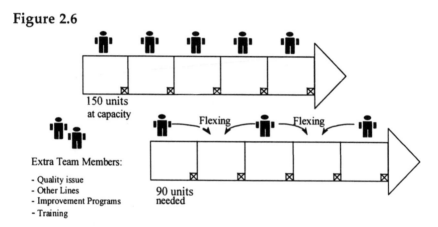

Some operations have what is known as a "jockey," or "floater." A jockey is someone who can do all the jobs, but is not assigned to a particular location. He or she can fill in for anyone when needed. The jockey may cover several lines and may perform other tasks, such as material handling or set-up preparation, when he or she is not filling in.

Scheduled breaks (including lunch) are always taken by the entire team, shutting down the entire line. This is a good time, by the way, to do preventative maintenance.

If an operator is going to be gone for more than a short time, on vacation as an example, the individual most likely will have to be replaced. Fortunately, in many countries where we have converted operations to lean, Europe and Latin America in particular, everyone goes on vacation at the same time. An entire plant is simply closed down. This is less disruptive than in the United States, where vacations are usually staggered.

*Job Satisfaction:* You may be wondering if there's a toll on people because they work more efficiently. Our experience has been that in all cases operators say they feel more relaxed, and can't believe they're producing at a higher rate. This is true even though throughput productivity normally increases by more than 30% once an operation coverts to continuous flow. Furthermore, by regularly changing what people do through the rotation of job assignments, workers experience a higher level of job satisfaction.

## A Brief Case Study

Let's look at a real life example of the results that were obtained in the implementation of continuous flow. Emission*Test* (fictitious name) produced a complicated device used to test car and truck exhaust emissions. The company employed more than 300 people, and was able to produce only about 1.5 devices per day. One glance at the manufacturing process was enough to see that it was disorganized. Parts never seemed to be where they were needed. People fought over resources and materials and guarded whatever they believed to be their turf. The business was in a financial crisis, having lost several hundred thousand dollars in the first 9 months of the year.

The customers of this company were irate. Some were preparing to sue because products had not been delivered as promised. One needed the product so badly, and had become so frustrated, that he actually was paying a consultant to help Emission*Test* find ways to become more productive. The consultant formed an internal team and went to work.

It was immediately obvious that continuous flow production was required, which would require breaking up the fiefdoms. The team mapped the process, and announced that the operation would shut down for two days while the entire plant was reconfigured. Needless to say, an uproar ensued, only to be calmed down by the company's desperate owner.

Machines were moved to produce a continuous flow assembly line, and an area for components inventory was created along with a kanban system to supply each workstation. Morning and afternoon production meetings were instituted as well, which forced everyone to begin communicating. No squabbling was allowed. Everyone was encouraged to focus on what would benefit customers. Back orders and how to get more units through the shop headed the list. Before long, catching up became a common goal, old barriers dissolved, and an atmosphere of cooperation replaced the rivalries. Personnel from one area were loaned out to those that needed a hand. Resources that would have been hoarded now were shared. In other words, the group had come together to form a team. In three weeks, production increased from 1.5 to 5 units per day with the result that the company shot out of the hole it had been in, and finished the year with a multi million dollar profit.

Continuous flow production and a team orientation (with a goal of customer satisfaction) transformed the group from individual fiefdoms into a unit. Bonds were formed. Walls came down. People worked together to get things moving, and to keep things moving. Improving customer satisfaction was the objective, but nearly a five-fold increase in productivity was the result.

### Instituting a Pull-Scheduling Kanban System

The kanban system is the key to linking customer demand to

all internal operations and, in turn, linking the company to the supply base. It might be compared to the nervous system of the lean producer, sending signals about what to produce, when, and in exactly what quantities. The kanban system is simple in concept, yet is one of the most misapplied elements of lean production. It communicates who is going to produce the product, where is it going to be stored, and it signals that the time has come to begin production. A kanban system also assumes a clearly defined process to be followed systematically by all.

The kanban system works on the simple principle of replenishment. When your customer uses a preset quantity of your product (or service), they send you a kanban (indicator) that tells you what to make, and that the time has come to make it. In this way, the customer is "pulling" the product from you at the rate it is being used. When your final assembly process consumes components and subassemblies, you send an internal kanban to an "upstream" operation to replenish what you used. When products from an outside supplier are consumed, a kanban order is sent to replace what was used. In this manner, all internal operations are tightly linked to customer demand and to suppliers with a minimal amount of inventory. Kanbans are the way a customer's takt time, the factory, and your suppliers all stay in sync.

Kanbans can take many different forms. The traditional kanban is a thick paper card that shows the part number, part description, usage location, and supply location. Figure 2.8 shows a kanban from Georgetown, Kentucky, where Toyota has more than 100,000 kanbans in circulation at any one time. The kanban shown is for ten seat belt assemblies. When Toyota team members

**Figure 2.6**

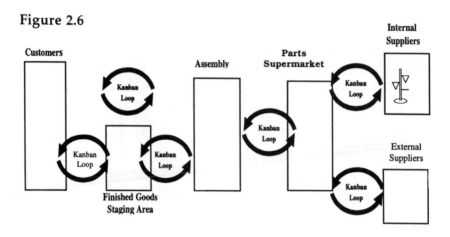

take the first seat belt out of the box, the kanban enters the replenishment cycle, making its way back to the supplier in about 36 hours. The supplier then produces the required replenishment quantity and puts it on a truck that takes it to Toyota 24 hours after the kanban was received. The total cycle time for replenishment, in this case, was 3 or 4 days, including shipping time. By contrast, the replenishment time for Toyota in Japan (where suppliers are often within one half hour of the Toyota factory) typically will be less than one day.

Figure 2.6, above, shows a typical pull scheduling system with kanbans. A kanban is not necessarily sent when the first element (a product) is taken out of the box. That will depend on the strategy that has been decided upon for the kanban process: A kanban card can be sent to the upstream process when the first element in a container is used, or when the last is used. It is important that once an approach is adopted, it is systematically applied throughout the entire kanban system.

A kanban might (figure 2.7) also be a bar-coded shipping label generated when a customer order is received. The shipping label in this case is a finished-goods kanban that starts the production process and ends up being attached to the goods for shipment. A

**Figure 2.7**

kanban can also be a parts bin. When an empty bin arrives, an operator knows he or she needs to replenish it. Alternatively, the signal to produce can also be a kanban square on the factory floor. A full square means no production is necessary, an empty square means production is required to fill it.

**Figure 2.8**

Whatever method is used, there are a few simple, but crucial principles that must be followed.

- Production should only be initiated with a kanban—no kanban, no production.
- Kanbans should be processed in the order in which they are received, on a "first come, first served" basis. The reason is that the entire lean production system is dependent on rapid replenishment of parts. Prioritization is set by usage—the more used, the more replenished. Remember also that the kanban system automatically corrects for scrap loss. If scrap rates are high in a downstream operation, it will pull more components from its upstream supplier as needed.
- Use a simple approach to determining the number of kanbans required for a given part number, then make incremental modifications. The number of kanbans in the system (including customer safety stocks) is determined by usage of finished goods and the replenishment time. If you use 1,000 of a given part per day, and it takes 3 days to replace the stock, then you need a minimum of 3,000 parts in the system. Practical realities also require a small safety margin of perhaps an additional several hours to 1 or 2 days of stocks in the system. If you are constantly running out of parts, it means there are not enough kanbans in the system and more need to be added. If there is an overabundance of parts, it means there are too many kanbans, and some should be removed. It is often best to have a larger number of bins/kanbans with fewer parts in each, rather than only 2 or 3 bins with a large number. Large bins make it difficult to adjust the number of kanbans in the system.

- Sometimes errors are made when determining the size of kanbans. For example, a supplier's lead time (time it takes from arrival of a kanban to fulfillment) is a week, but the supplier delivers everyday. One may be tempted to size kanbans based on replenishment time (lead time). But, since the supplier can deliver everyday, it would be more convenient to lower kanban sizes and have five kanbans at any time at the supplier's site. A substantially lower inventory of the particular part would be the result.

- Storage of intermediate assemblies, components, and raw materials must follow rigid first in, first out (FIFO) rules. This has more to do with quality than with kanbans themselves. If a quality problem is detected, the bad parts need to be removed from the production process. By having a FIFO system, you can generally tell the starting point and ending point of the bad parts in the system. Otherwise, if parts are intermingled, you would have to sort or scrap all parts in the system.

**Figure 2.9**

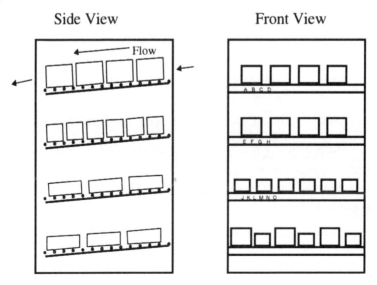

**Figure 2.10**

Many systems can be devised to ensure that the first parts produced are the first to be used. Figure 2.9 on page 129 illustrates a flow-through rack system that ensures FIFO. Parts bins are loaded from the back and pulled from the front. Figure 2.10 illustrates a less expensive solution. Containers are fed from one side and taken from another. Another inexpensive system is to place an arrow on a wire stretched over columns of stock. As stock is used up, the arrow is moved to the right, indicating what should be used next. Replenishment occurs in the empty column. More on FIFO relating to quality is discussed in Part III.

### The Start of the "Pull" Process, The Customer Link

The kanban link to the customer sets the stage for the entire kanban process in a company. This is often left to the end of the installation of a kanban system. In fact, it should be done at the beginning.

There are three basic approaches (or models) that can be taken to the customer interface. There is no right or wrong as long as kanban principles are followed. Here are a few examples.

## Model 1. Customer Kanban Link to Small Finished Goods Staging Area

This is the classic Toyota system approach. The customer sends a kanban (similar to the Toyota kanban in Figure 2.7) to the supplier to replenish products it has consumed. The product is pulled from the finished goods staging area, and is shipped to the customer on the next delivery. In the meantime, an internal kanban is sent back to the final manufacturing stage of the factory to replenish the staging area. This approach is typical of a Toyota group supplier. For the seat belt producer we mentioned above, order lead time from Toyota was 24 hours; the staging area had about 0.5 to 1.5 days of supply, depending on the volatility of demand. Their counterparts in Japan had a lead time of four hours, with a staging area of about eight hours' supply.

The actual kanban from the customer can be in the form of a card, an empty bin, a fax, or an Electronic Data Interchange (EDI) release. The physical form of the kanban is not important.

This method of kanban linkage to the customer is most often used when the order-to-ship lead time is short (e.g. hours to 1-2 days) and is about the same time as the manufacturing replenishment process.

**Figure 2.11, First In, First Out (FIFO)**

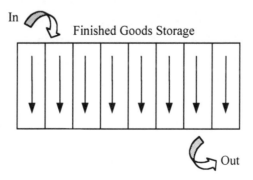

The staging area is always organized on a visual basis with dedicated areas for each finished goods part number and rigid first-in-first-out control.

## Model 2. Customer Kanban Link Direct to Factory Order

This type of customer kanban linkage is becoming more popular. It makes efficient use of company assets since virtually no finished goods inventory exists (other than product waiting to be shipped). It is generally used when the order lead time is sufficiently longer than the manufacturing replenishment cycle, so that a safety stock of finished goods is not required. Dell Computer uses this direct link approach to its customer orders when they come over the Internet, as described in Part I.

Let's return to the seat belt producer example. Several of its customers issued a one-week firm order, with shipments every day, or every other day. In this case, the orders were received via EDI directly into Production Control (PC). PC reviewed the order to ensure there were no blatant errors (occasionally, for example, a customer mistakenly would order several weeks supply in a single shipment) and would communicate with the customer if any problems were found. When the order was okay (about 95% of the time), it was sent to a bar-code printer that printed the shipping labels for the order. The shipping labels served as the finished good kanban to initiate the manufacturing process. It is important to note that all 5 days of kanbans were issued to the assembly-line team leaders on the factory floor. The team leaders scheduled production to meet the customer delivery schedule. Each cell using this system had a production board with hooks for each day of the week. The kanbans for each day's deliveries were placed on the hooks so that everyone on the cell knew exactly how the cell was doing in terms of meeting the customer requirements.

There were a few rules each cell needed to follow: First, they had to build in "shipment packs," i.e. the precise quantity and mix of product that the customer wanted in a given shipment. Generally, this meant that each assembly cell made every product, every day. The teams were allowed to build ahead approximately one day in order to maintain a small safety stock. For example, Wednesday morning's shipment would be completed by the end of second shift on Monday evening. Second, the team leaders did their own leveling of the production schedule. If the actual shipment quantity varied from day to day, the team leader would take the average of the daily shipments and produce the same amount every day. Third, since the shop-floor teams were responsible for meeting the customer's delivery requirements, they made their own decisions about whether or not to work overtime. Customer satisfaction was the goal.

## Model 3. Orders for Rarely Produced Items—the One-time Kanban

In many cases, certain items are ordered infrequently, say every few months, in unpredictable quantities. In such instances it may not be economical to maintain finished goods safety stock or intermediate subassemblies in the manufacturing process. This is where a one-time kanban can be used, which calls for special production of an item. Typically, the kanban will have a different color or appearance for easy identification. When it is issued to the final assembly cell, the team leader will place it in a segregated section of the scheduling board, and will also send one-time kanbans backward into the production process to make any parts or subassemblies that are not kept in internal stocks. If materials and components are required from outside suppliers, they are ordered as well. Sometimes this process is done by simultaneously issuing internal and external orders for all components directly from production control (similar to conventional shop-floor order processing methods).

The three main methods of linking customers with your company—used individually or in combination—will cover most situations. Let's look at some variations on the models.

### Distributor Orders with Multiple Line Items

What do you do if you supply distributors, not OEMs, and their orders vary significantly in terms of frequency, quantity, number of line items, and product mix? If your business model requires near instantaneous turnaround of those orders (say that you must ship in a few hours), then you will probably need a finished goods staging area from which the order is picked for shipment. The order would be transmitted from the point of order entry directly to the shipping area; the order would be picked and assembled; then internal kanbans would be sent back to the factory to produce stock for replenishment. This is essentially a slight modification of the Model 1 approach discussed above.

If, however, you have a bit more time to fill the order (let's say a day or two), then you can use a variation of Model 2. In this case, the order entry process will need to issue internal kanbans to each manufacturing cell that needs to produce the product. As with the seat belt manufacturer, each assembly cell or area would have a master scheduling board (called a heijunka box by Toyota) where the backlog of orders can be easily seen. Each kanban will have to be identified with a specific distributor order so it can be matched up with other line items before shipment.

At the same time that the kanbans are released to the shop floor, a manifest or some other document would be issued to the shipping department where a staging area would be established for the assembly of the shipment. Once all the line items are received, the order is packed and shipped.

Note that, so far, the order entry systems are simple and do not require elaborate computer systems. Often, a manual system or a PC with a spreadsheet are adequate. In the case of the seat belt manufacturer, an external EDI mailbox system (provided by an outside vendor) was linked via modem to a PC and the PC was in turn linked to a bar-code printer. There was a small amount of custom programming to display and format the orders and to interface with the company's financial system. Elaborate MRP II planning systems are simply not required. (More is coming later on this subject.)

### Dealing With Highly Erratic Customer Orders

A common excuse for not installing a kanban link to the customer is that the customer's orders are highly erratic and unpredictable. Usually, this situation is due to the customer's MRP system, which is batch and queue oriented. When the customer's MRP volatility interacts with your own company's MRP, the result can be true chaos on the shop floor. In the longer term, you will want to sell your customer on the advantages of a direct kanban linkage. This is generally not practical, of course, when you are just starting on the lean journey (mainly because the customer won't listen).

Suppose a customer issues a multi-week shipment schedule. The first task is to determine how much of the schedule is a firm commitment. Our experience has been that the truly firm portion of the schedule is seldom more than one week. Despite a customer talking about a firm commitment, they will usually make changes during the next release that will effect shipments that are one week away or more. The other reason for the one-week horizon is that companies will often run their MRP systems once per week.

Let's assume that the one-week commitment is the appropriate horizon. In this case, Production Control would issue a week's worth of orders to the team leaders on the shop floor, the same as

Model 2 above. The team on the floor then does their own scheduling to meet the customer requirement.

It is important to add a sanity check to customer's orders when making the transition to the pull system. First, it is important to know the customer's actual assembly line rates (OEM customers) because you will often receive orders that exceed your capacity and the customer's capacity. Here again is chaos introduced by MRP. Since you cannot fill an order that exceeds your capacity, it is necessary to discuss the situation with your customer and attempt to change the order. Here's where knowing the customer's line rates comes into play. Since they can't possibly consume the parts ordered, why not change it to something more reasonable and also reduce their in-house inventory?

In spite of the potential difficulties of installing a pull system in an erratic customer ordering situation, you will still be better off to do so than if you try to plan and forecast for erratic orders. The latter situation is truly hopeless, and tends to drive your suppliers crazy because your MRP system will amplify the problems back through the supply chain.

A key role of the sales department here will be to sell the pull system concept to the customer. Your customer establishes kanban squares on its factory floor and pulls from that stock as needed. You then replenish the stock within an agreed upon lead time. Think of the competitive advantage you will have as you work that replenishment time down from a week to a few days to perhaps a few hours. Your competition, if it is not lean, can only follow by using huge amounts of inventory.

Often, when a process such as this is sold to a customer, there's a temporary reduction in orders. This will last until the customer's inventory is reduced to levels that are compatible with your new delivery schedule. The situation is, however, temporary and will disappear as a customer's inventory is reduced. Nevertheless, if you are subject to monthly operations reviews, this may present a problem for you. It will be important to have this discussed and understood by all in advance.

Now let's work our way backward, using kanbans to pull components and subassemblies from internal operations and from suppliers.

### Internal Component and Subassembly Kanbans

Let us assume that we have a continuous-flow, final assembly process that is linked to a customer's demand. How do you keep the necessary materials flowing to the line? We will do so with internal and supplier kanbans, which are really no different in concept than the kanbans linked to the customer. As before, the internal kanban can be in the form of a card, a bin, an empty square, or a bar-coded label—anything that signals that replenishment is necessary. The rules for determining the number of kanbans for a given component are the same as described earlier—the average daily usage multiplied by the replenishment time (e.g. days or fractions of days, taking into consideration shorter delivery times for suppliers that have delivery times different than their lead times). An additional safety stock may be needed to cover volatility and unexpected situations. A larger number of kanbans, each with smaller quantities makes adjustment of the inventory levels easier than only two or three kanbans, each with a large quantity.

Whenever a break in a continuous flow operation occurs, a kanban system to link it to the next upstream operation will be needed. Obviously, if the entire factory were a single line from the receiving dock to shipment, internal kanbans would not be needed. But such a situation is seldom practical. Usually there will be small internal buffer stock, called a supermarket, in-between final assembly operations and upstream supplies. The final assembly operations pull from the supermarket, and a replenishment order is sent from the supermarket to the supplying department (e.g. injection molding, stamping, plating, auto-insertion for electronic components).

Supermarkets are set up to be highly visible and "in the flow" of the factory. They also must follow rigid first-in-first-out principals for quality control purposes. Over time, as replenishment times get shorter, the amount of stock in the supermarket will steadily diminish. In one of the operations where we worked, the entire internal supermarket has about one-half to one day of supply. (Later, we will discuss rapid set-up time, which is crucial to maintaining small supermarkets.)

*Signal kanbans:* The signal kanban below is a special form of kanban often used for batch operations (e.g. injection molding, stamping, or plating). It is essentially a reorder point system and

**Figure 2.12** **Signal Kanban**

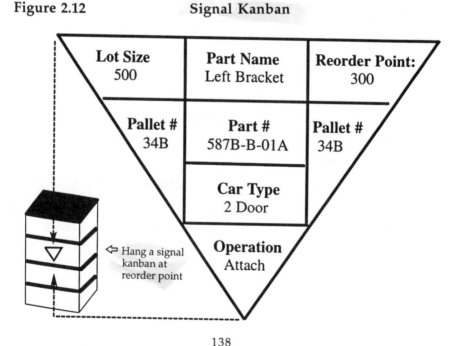

can be used instead of individual cards or bins. The seat belt supplier mentioned earlier uses a signal kanban for its internal injection molding operations. The signal would be set at the minimum quantity of buffer stock for a given part. When the bin is removed from the supermarket, the attached signal kanban is put on a kanban tree that tells the molding machine operator what to produce next. The kanban contains all the information the operator needs to know about the part including the assigned machine, the batch size, the process control program for the machine, and the storage location for the molded parts. A signal kanban is not a requirement for batch operations; it is merely an alternative to individual cards and/or bins.

*A Special Problem—Sequential Batch Operations:* Many plants with older equipment will require a series of batch operations to produce a given component—for example, stamping, followed by heat treating and/or plating. In such a situation there are essentially two choices: Establish supermarkets between each operation, or treat the series of operations as if they all were one continuous flow. Figure 2.13 compares the two.

**Figure 2.13**

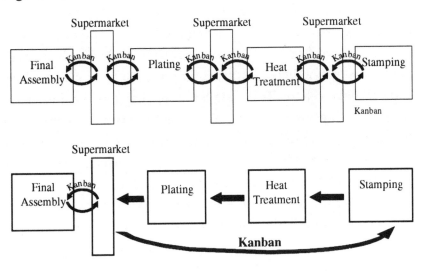

The supermarket approach is simple to operate and provides rapid replenishment to the operations consuming the parts. It increases the amount of WIP inventory, which consumes capital and floor space. The continuous flow approach generally requires less WIP inventory and floor space, but it has two disadvantages: (1) a longer replenishment time, and (2) a routing slip to be attached to each kanban that defines the series of operations needed (not too different from traditional shop orders). An older plant we know of selected the continuous flow approach. It has a five-day replenishment cycle for parts that are stamped, heat treated and plated, which may be at the outer limit of feasibility.

The longer-term approach is to downsize batch equipment and reduce replenishment time. We found in one case that it was cheaper to use a stainless steel stamping than plated carbon steel. The part could go directly from stamping to assembly.

The approach to be taken for batch operations must be made on an individual basis, weighing the parameters described above. As lean implementation progresses, it is advantageous to put some batch operations right into the final assembly process. We have seen this done with stamping presses, injection molding machines, and automatic insertion for electronic components.

*Case Study:* One plant had four final assembly lines to make energy regulators. After converting the lines to continuous flow, output jumped from 1,400 units per shift to 1,600. The lines were now, however, allegedly outstripping the capacity of the single subassembly cell (called a staker line) that fed the four final assembly lines with electrical contact housings. Some lines frequently ran out of housings, and when this happened, the line would go down. The situation had become chaotic. There were squabbles between workers, and scavenging for parts.

We studied the situation and saw that one tray of staked housings lasted a line an hour. It took 15 minutes for the staker line to replace a tray, and there were four lines being fed. The staker line should have been able to supply them all.

The product being made on each line had a code. We used this to create a kanban card for each. Then we put up a board with a peg. Whenever a product line was finished with a tray, the material handler now would take the card from the tray and put it behind those already on the peg. In this way, kanbans governed which type of housing would be staked next. Since each batch took fifteen minutes to replace, and each batch lasted an hour, no line now ran out of housings. When a batch was completed, the card was put with it on the tray and taken to the appropriate line. Around and around it went. Output eventually climbed from 1,600 per line to 2,200 units, with the original staker line easily keeping pace.

### Kanban Interface with the Supply Base

Many companies making the mass-to-lean transformation feel somewhat trapped between an unenlightened customer and an unenlightened supply base. This is especially true in a world driven by dueling MRP systems that can lead to logistics chaos. We remember trying to use card kanbans with the seat belt manufacturer's supply base—only to find that the suppliers didn't understand the purpose of the kanbans and tended to lose them regularly, not realizing that each lost kanban is a lost order.

So what is the solution? First, the principles of kanban interface with the supply base are identical to the interface with customers and internal operations. Training of the suppliers in kanban methods is required.

Here is how the system for the seat belt supplier mentioned above worked. Each bin of components from a supplier had an AIAG (Automotive Industry Action Group) standard shipping label that was shipped with the parts. When the parts were used by the assembly cell, the operator scanned the component kanban (the parts' shipping label) which generated a pull order to the internal warehouse and to the supplier. These replenishment orders were filled immediately from the internal staging area, and were also queued (in the computer). Each evening, the orders were sent to the suppliers via fax or EDI. When suppliers shipped the parts, they included the AIAG label that served as both shipping label and replenishment kanban. When the parts were received at the seat belt manufacturer, the master bar codes were scanned to electronically receive the parts and add them to inventory. The system also flagged any items that required incoming inspection before they could be put into the staging area. Once the parts were received, a signal was sent to Accounts Payable with an authorization to pay the supplier on whatever terms had been agreed to. Therefore, this system also eliminated the messy paperwork of invoicing. The supplier was paid based on good parts received.

There was another, but critical aspect of the seat belt manufacturer's system. Because the seat belt manufacturer was making a safety-related product (seat belts), a component lot tracing system was critical. Each kanban also contained a lot tracing code that was captured each time the kanban was scanned. In this manner, the specific lot codes of components could be tracked throughout the production process. This was crucial in the event a component problem was detected. It would be then essential to know which assemblies had components that were potentially at risk.

The only difference between this system and a normal kanban system is that the return loop to the supplier is electronic, rather than a package of card kanbans that is delivered physically. The electronic return loop is also faster.

Is it necessary to have this type of electronic system? No. Any of the manual methods used internally can also work with suppliers. With proper training, cards and bins work fine. We've also seen situations where internal kanbans were accumulated and transferred to a fax order, then transmitted to the supplier. We have, in fact, developed a bias for simple electronic solutions such as this because there is always a chance that cards and bins may get lost.

## Kanban Maintenance

Kanban maintenance is often misunderstood and neglected. First, it is important to know at all times how many kanbans are in the system so that kanbans can be added or deleted to maintain optimum safety stock levels. Second, when a part number changes (say from Revision A to Revision B), all the kanbans from Revision A must be removed from the system as the A parts are consumed, and B-level kanbans substituted in their place. Third, care must be taken to ensure that kanbans are not lost. Each lost kanban represents a reduction of inventory and the creation of a potential stock-out situation. You always want to remove kanbans deliberately, not accidentally.

This leads to an interesting anecdote. We discovered in one operation that kanban control and maintenance was poor and stock-outs and over-supply were occurring too frequently. Upon investigation, it was determined that the team leaders on the assembly floor were hoarding kanbans in their desks. Whenever they were short of parts, they would introduce an extra kanban and would keep a couple in reserve when new parts arrived. The head of operations declared a "Kanban Amnesty Day" where anyone could turn in their kanbans with no questions asked. He put a large cardboard box on his desk, and left the plant for two shifts. When he came back the next morning, the box was full. The source of the kanban control problem had been discovered.

Obviously, this incident reflected a deeper problem, i.e., lack of understanding on the part of team leaders of how the system worked. A new and more rigorous round of training was initiated, and the problem did not resurface.

Another aspect of kanban maintenance relates to the supplier orders. It is imperative to maintain a log of kanban orders that are sent to suppliers, along with expected delivery dates. Supply problems will still occur even with a kanban system.

We recommend starting with a manual kanban system during the early stages of the lean transformation. The reason is that it can be installed quickly and easily and valuable experience can be gained early in the process. In the medium and long term, however, an electronic system using bar coded labels is preferable from a control and maintenance point of view.

## Beware the Green, Yellow, Red Scheduling Board

Multicolored production control boards are often used when there are multiple kanbans for multiple parts circulating in a system. These boards are supposed to set production priorities. The colors are used to signal the level of urgency for the production of a component. Normally, a board is employed that has three colors, and kanban cards are collected in the appropriate columns. The level of urgency for each is communicated by the color of the row in which it is placed. For example, if kanbans are in the red, this indicates these products need to be made before those in yellow. What happens, however, if there is a sudden shift in demand? Priority will change as well. Unless a mechanism is in place that adjusts row colors accordingly, a situation could occur in which a product is in green (low priority) status, and the user of that part is waiting impatiently for it to arrive. So, a critically-needed state can be reached without the producing stations being made aware.

The conceptual flaw in this system is that it violates one of the key principals of the kanban system. Kanbans must be replenished as soon as possible. They need to follow a first come, first served philosophy in order to ensure continued supply at the next stage of production. The scheduling of a component should *not* be done based on how many kanbans are in a system. Otherwise, a component that has "too many" kanbans in the system will be automatically relegated to a lower priority. The impression at the consuming location will in fact be that there are not enough kanbans. Otherwise, the replenishment time could be dramatically slowed if the supplying department is busy.

## Kanban and MRP

The kanban system replaces MRP for shop floor control. Kanbans synchronize internal production to the customer demand like a Swiss watch. Kanban pull scheduling is also much simpler in concept and practice than MRP. Many MRP vendors will replace their shop floor orders with something they call a kanban and declare that this is a lean system. Do not be fooled. Kanbans and MRP are completely incompatible for shop floor control.

Is there a role for MRP at all in a pull scheduling system? The answer is yes. MRP should be used for the purpose for which it was originally intended—*planning*. Even in a pull-scheduling environment, it is necessary to forecast material and capacity requirements, both inside the company and for suppliers. This is an ideal role for the planning capabilities of MRP, which can be linked to a kanban system as shown in Figure 2.14 that appears on the page that follows.

**Figure 2.14**

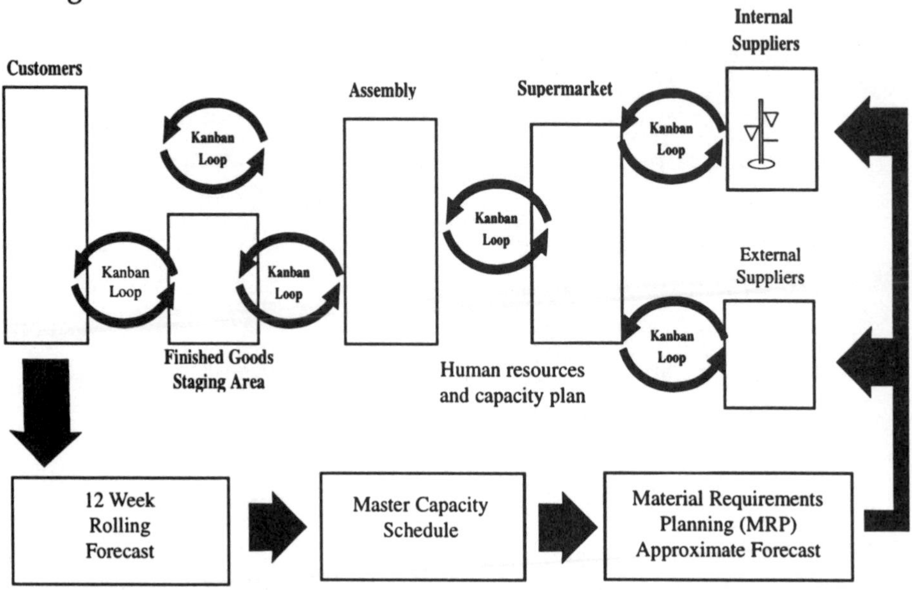

Forecasts from customers and internal forecasts drive a master capacity schedule that is used to determine internal capacity and manpower requirements. The capacity needed can either be built into the MRP system, or it is also possible to simply print out the production requirements for the next few months and let the team leaders do the capacity/manpower analyses.

It is also important to communicate material needs to the supply base so that it also knows approximately what production will be required. We typically see the MRP bill of material (BOM) explosion carried out for about three months and given to the suppliers as a planning tool. It can also be used as authorization for suppliers to procure their own long-lead material supplies. The suppliers must understand, however, that the plan represents only an approximation. The actual release for a shipment will only come by kanban (with one exception discussed next).

## Items That Have Long Lead Times

Items with long lead times (say more than eight to ten weeks) require special consideration. A kanban system can be used for replenishing these parts, but it is important to realize that kanban begins to lose effectiveness as lead times stretch out. Suppose, for example, a part has a lead time of ten weeks. When you consume that part today, a kanban signal is sent to the supplier and a replacement shows up ten weeks later. The implicit assumption is that your consumption rate ten weeks from now will be the same as it is today. This is not always valid, and either over-supply or a shortage of parts can be a result. In this situation, it can be better to order the long-lead items from an MRP forecast. If only a limited number of parts are involved (let's say less than 5% of the total number of line items), and they are managed with a high degree of scrutiny, the problem of long-lead parts can be effectively solved.

In the final analysis, no need exists for MRP scheduling on the shop floor.

## Keeping the Lines Running—Maintenance Programs

Let's assume that you are now up and running in a continuous flow operation. All your processes are linked together with virtually no inventory between them. When one machine goes down in the process, the entire line goes down. This is when the people who do not want to transform to lean will say "See, we told you this wouldn't work. Now we can't keep the lines running. The factory is going to shut down!"

Two issues need to be addressed immediately as part of the lean transformation: (1) Having maintenance immediately available to fix a machine that is down, and (2) A total productive maintenance (TPM) program which includes regular, preventative maintenance to minimize unscheduled downtime.

*Total Productive Maintenance:* This program addresses four fundamental aspects of the overall maintenance picture: Routine maintenance, preventative maintenance, predictive maintenance and immediate (corrective) maintenance. It is a comprehensive, all inclusive, program whose sole objective is ensuring that there is no time wasted due to machine failure or malfunction.

*Immediate Maintenance Support:* Repair personnel must be available on a moment's notice. A common method of signaling a downed line is an "andon light." Each continuous flow line or cell will have a bank of three lights, green means everything is running okay, yellow means that there is a material shortage, and red means that the line is down due to a machine problem, and immediate maintenance help is needed. A red light means that the maintenance person assigned to the line (or one of his or her colleagues) must stop whatever they are doing and service the line. Response time should be one to two minutes. We've also seen more sophisticated approaches to call for maintenance support. Radios or pagers can be used to signal for help. In some plants, the need for help is entered into computer and the request prints out immediately in the maintenance department. No matter how notification is handled, it is important to have people on hand and ready to drop what they are doing and tend to a machine on the blink.

As the number of lines are converted, more pressure will be put on maintenance and repair personnel. As a result, the maintenance department in your business may have to expand.

You also are likely to discover that spare parts inventories need to be thoroughly reviewed. If your experience holds true to form, you will probably have lots of parts you don't need, and will be missing the ones you need most. None of this will have been visible when you had piles of inventory. Then, you could afford to have a machine down for a few days waiting for parts.

Now you can't afford for it to be down more than a few minutes.

Also, you'll want to give consideration to the scheduling of breaks. Not all of the maintenance staff should go to lunch or take breaks at the same time. Someone must be available in the event of trouble. Nor should maintenance staff have breaks at the same time as machine operators. The time to service machines is when they're not in use. Staggering lunch breaks, for example, can make it possible for maintenance to be performed while operators are away.

Staggering breaks may make sense for other reasons as well. For example, everyone went to lunch at the same time at a plant in Europe. This plant made an item that had a printed dial. The printing process requires two machines. When lunch time came, the ink had to be removed and cleaned from all the surfaces or it would dry out. When people returned, both machines had to be re-inked, which took twenty minutes. While this was taking place, others on the line waited around with nothing to do. The solution was simple: stagger lunch breaks so that the machines are never stopped. The resulting increase in productivity was staggering.

Perhaps this seems obvious. It was, of course, but this kind of waste goes on all the time in many organizations. It often is caused simply because something has always been done a certain way. After a while, the routine becomes a habit that no one questions. Herein lies one of the values of converting to lean. When you undergo transformation, you'll be forced to think out of the box. You'll see things in a new light, and this can pay big dividends.

It may also be helpful to bring someone in from the outside to observe an operation with a fresh pair of eyes. An outsider will often see things that have a tendency to blend into the background once they have become routine.

While immediate response to machine downtime is crucial, it is better if machinery does not break down in the first place. This leads us to the need for a thorough and rigorous *preventative maintenance* program that covers every piece of machinery in the facility. This is the only way to get out of the "fire-fighting" mode of only responding to breakdowns.

In a TPM *(Total Productive Maintenance)* program, every machine has a preventative maintenance schedule to ensure that it never breaks down unexpectedly. Spare parts supplies are maintained for items that need to be changed regularly. Usually, a computer system will be used to track the TPM program.

One of the companies we worked with has one of the most sophisticated systems we've seen where every machine has a maintenance schedule and a log of what's been performed (as well as any unscheduled downtime). Any overdue items are immediately highlighted by the system and are a cause for near-term action as soon as the machine is available to be worked on. Each machine has a performance chart that is also used to help predict when a breakdown might occur.

We have observed that preventative maintenance is generally quite poor in most mass production organizations. When lots of inventory exists, the lost production capacity from a machine going down is often not obvious. We've heard comments like "Machine A is down again, but its okay since we have several weeks of inventory." People adopt a wait-until-it-breaks-down philosophy, and almost view preventative maintenance as an unaffordable luxury. In fact, the opposite is true of a lean producer. The cost of running a continuous flow cell can often be several hundred dollars per hour (or more). Unexpected downtime is costly.

Here is a real-life example of a "penny wise and pound foolish" approach to preventative maintenance at an electronics assembly facility. Each assembled board was tested with a in-circuit tester toward the end of the cell. The testers used a $50 rubberized gasket to ensure a good vacuum seal to hold the circuit board against the test pins. After several months, the gaskets would wear out, causing leaks in the vacuum. The result was a lot of false rejections of good circuit boards, unnecessary rework, and an eventual breakdown of the machine. The gaskets were deemed to be too expensive to have in stock, and definitely too expensive to replace on a scheduled basis. This assembly cell cost about $500 per hour to run, including direct costs and depreciation. So the cost of one gasket was covered in less than 10 minutes of downtime. While this example shows the case for preventative maintenance in the extreme, it is not that unusual.

It is not our objective to provide a tutorial on preventative maintenance and TPM programs. There are many good texts and training programs available. The key point here is that general managers and plant managers must recognize the critical need for preventative maintenance and must ensure that it be done.

*Predictive Maintenance:* This is an activity seldom employed that can provide important benefits in assuring that a production facility does not experience lost time due to machine failure or malfunctioning. The idea is to predict a potential failure before it occurs. A system is established that uses measurement and analysis techniques that allow predicting a potential failure. Let's look at an example. Consider an automatic insertion machine that is used to insert axial or radial electronic components in a printed circuit board. Let's say that in a specific board process, an increase in missed insertions clearly occurs as time goes by. This may be an indication that an insertion head is wearing out, and may need to be replaced. By being proactive, maintenance can be performed when the machine is not in use. The machine can be checked, and if the head indeed needs replacement, it can be done without disrupting regularly scheduled work. By charting occurrences such as this, the maintenance organization can develop a predictive program that will, over time, minimize machine downtime. We have found that operators can play a key role in the development of a program such as this if they are coached to be sensitive to subtle changes in the performance of the machines they operate.

*Routine Maintenance:* This activity refers to actions to be performed daily by operators and maintenance personnel. Many times these activities are relegated to a secondary role, and are only done if there is time available at the end of the day.

In one of the facilities where we worked, a delicate situation existed with equipment on a semi-automatic line. A malfunction seemed to occur every other minute. In most cases, these malfunctions had to do with an automatic feeder. Components would become blocked and cause the machine to stop. In an effort to stem this problem, operators and maintenance personnel began to include in their daily routine the complete cleaning of all feeders, including feeding tubes and vibrator beds. Once this program was undertaken, stoppages virtually ended.

Routine maintenance needs to be a regularly scheduled chore undertaken daily. In some instances, it should be done more than once per day. Maintenance should be scheduled, and operators should be trained to perform it.

At least six factors can hold down performance, including: (1) downtime due to breaks, (2) downtime of short duration due to jams, (3) machine or line speed losses, (4) line and/or machine setup losses, (5) production of defective products that result in scrap or rework and (6) startup issues.

A good way to keep tabs on the TPM program is to chart machine performance, often referred to as Overall Equipment Effectiveness (OEE). A formula might be developed that combines downtime due to factors listed above into an index, which can then be tracked so that goals can be established and progress measured. Whatever method is used, measurements need to remain consistent over time.

## Quick Changeover

As has been mentioned, rapid changeover from one part to another is critical to maintaining continuous flow production. Unfortunately, for most mass manufacturers, reduction of setup time has not been a major priority. If, for example, a stamping press takes several hours to set up, a larger batch size would be produced to minimize the impact of a long setup time. In a lean environment, this approach does not work because: (1) you will have far too much inventory and (2) replenishment time for a given part will be much too long.

To stay with the stamping press example, let's say that a press takes 2 hours to set up. Because of the long setup, you want to run it for at least 14 hours to make the changeover economical. Therefore, you are making one part per day (two shifts). If the stamping press makes six different parts, your replenishment time will be six days, and you will have at least a six-day supply of each part (probably you will have several weeks' supply of each). Conversely, if your setup time is ten minutes, you can make all six parts every day with the same amount of total setup time (one hour)—and your inventory will be a fraction of what it was since your replenishment time is now less than one day.

We have been using the following rules of thumb—changeovers should be made in less than ten minutes for batch operations and should be made in one takt time for final assembly operations. At the seat belt manufacturer, injection molding machines were changed over in four to eight minutes, including material and/or color change. Assembly lines were changed over in 30 seconds.

How is this possible? In the case of injection molding, all

molds had quick disconnect fixtures on the water lines. The molds were sitting on a cart next to the machine. Special hoppers had been designed to minimize the amount of material in the machine. All tools needed for the changeover were available prior to making the change. The molding machines had pre-stored programs for each part, and the operators were trained in rapid changeover procedures. For final assembly cells, all parts were available for the changeover. All work instructions were color-coded and were available at all times at each station. All test machines had built-in programs that could be changed with a selector switch, and the operators were trained in rapid change procedures.

We need to clarify that when we refer to change over time, we are referring to time it takes from the last good part made to the first good part made. A changeover actually may take more than 10 minutes, but if the majority of the activities are conducted off line (that is without interrupting the normal functioning of the machine), the interruption of normal operations could be less than 10 minutes. This is referred to as external set up (external to the machine, causing no interruption of normal functioning).

Most companies deal with the setup time issue early in the lean transformation. In final assembly, the pain of a long changeover will rob the company of productive hours. In the case of batch operations, long setups will result in much larger inventory buffers than are desirable. Even if setup times are long, it's better to start the pull scheduling process and, in parallel, begin a setup reduction program. As setups become shorter, the organization will see huge amounts of inventory melt away.

For those who think it can't be done, consider the following. Toyota will typically change the stamping dies for automotive body panels in less than ten minutes. The dies are the size of a car, and the presses about five times larger yet. The die change routine is carefully choreographed. After the last stroke of the previous part, hydraulic clamps release the die and it is moved aside on rollers. At the same time, the new die is moved into place. Automatic guides align the new die, and the press is gently closed. Hydraulic clamps are closed to secure the new die into place. After several alignment and safety checks, the press is ready to stamp out the new body panel.

Many excellent texts have been written on quick setups. (Probably one of the best is Shigeo Shingo's *A Revolution in Manufacturing: The SMED System.*) A common sense set of guidelines, includes the following:

- Before making a changeover, ensure that all items necessary for the changeover are at hand (e.g. all tools, safety equipment, cranes, the die or mold itself, procedures, machine settings, and so on).
- Make sure all dies, molds, etc., for a given machine have the same dimensions to minimize extra adjustments.
- Make use of quick disconnect devices for hoses, clamps, etc., that are required.
- Have all work instructions for the new part at hand.
- Have any "first off" quality checks made immediately, preferably at or near the machine itself. The seat belt manufacturer we discussed earlier, performed dimensional checks on the first parts after a mold change. The optical comparator used for this purpose was in the center of the molding department.
- Conduct all possible activities external to the process prior to interrupting the normal functioning of a machine. An example would be the external heating of a hot die for a plastic injection molding machine.

We suggest that you get together with all the parties involved and brainstorm ways to speed along the changeover process. It is often helpful to video tape a setup, and then play it back to the personnel involved so that they can look for opportunities for improvement. In almost all instances, big gains can be realized with little, if any, outlay of capital.

## Six Sigma Quality

Most traditional companies believe that 99.9% good quality is a terrific achievement. Perhaps by historical standards it is. However, consider what 99.9% good quality would mean in everyday life in the United States:

- Unsafe drinking water once per week
- No electricity for nearly one hour per month
- 500 wrong surgical procedures per week
- 2 short or long landings at most airports each week
- 20,000 wrong drug prescriptions per year
- 2,000 lost articles of mail per hour

Perhaps 99.9% is not so good, after all.

World class companies ship products to their customers with 99.99966% good quality. From a statistical point of view, this means that they are shipping six sigma quality—no more than 3.4 parts per million defects. This is nearly zero.

The term six sigma (also written 6 σ, using the lower case Greek letter for sigma), refers to the number of standard deviations away from the mean (or average) point in a bell curve (also known as a "normal distribution").

For readers who are not statisticians, the bell curve is a natural phenomenon experienced in large populations of almost anything. Imagine, for example that you are harvesting corn. The size of most of the ears will be centered around the mean (average) of the population. A few ears will be moderately large and fewer still will be very large. The same relationship appears in the smaller sizes—a moderate number are smaller than the mean, and a still smaller number are very small. If a million ears are harvested, only three to four ears will fall in the very largest category (six sigma from the mean) and only 3-4 ears will fall into the smallest category (six sigma from the mean in the other direction). The size of all the other ears will fall into a "normal distribution" as defined by the bell curve shown below in Figure 2.15. This same relationship tends to hold for populations of people. If the height or weight of a large population is measured and plotted on a graph, the statistics will fall into the classical normal distribution.

**Figure 2.15**

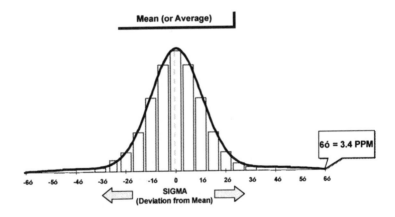

In manufacturing, the naturally occurring variations in processes will also tend to fall into a normal distribution, for example, the dimensions of stamped or injected-molded parts, the thickness of plating, or the amount of solder on a printed circuit board.

Achieving six sigma delivered quality to the customer is not an easy feat, especially considering the rolled throughput yield where

**Figure 2.16**

| σ Level | % Good Quality | % Defects | PPM Defects |
|---------|----------------|-----------|-------------|
| 2 | 69.1% | 30.9% | 308,537 |
| 3 | 93.3% | 6.7% | 66,807 |
| 4 | 99.4% | 0.64% | 6,210 |
| 5 | 99.98% | 0.02% | 233 |
| 6 | 99.9997% | 0.00034% | 3.4 |

the yields of each sequential processes are multiplied together to compute the final yield.[26] For example, if there are four processes, each with a 99% yield, the rolled throughput yield is (0.99)x(0.99)x(0.99)x(0.99) = 96%.

So how do world class companies achieve such a small amount of defects delivered to the customer? A combination of methods are used that ensure that a defect is rarely passed on to the next stage of production. Let's look at some of the methods.

### Operator Responsibility for Quality

Whenever we go into a factory, we ask the operators on the shop floor, "Who is responsible for quality?"

A surprising number will respond, "The Quality Department" i.e., the operators do not take responsibility for the quality of what they do because a quality inspector will verify their work.

If you ask the same question in a lean factory, you will always get the answer, "I am" or "We are all responsible for quality." This philosophy is probably the most important determinant of whether a company will or will not deliver high defects.

One factory with which we worked had a quality inspection function and a quality audit function to check the outgoing quality of final assembly. In spite of this double-inspection approach, about 5% to 10% of audited product was found to be out of specification, and the customer saw several thousand parts per million in defects. Obviously, the system was not working. As a result, the general manager of the facility eliminated final inspection and put the responsibility for quality in the hands of the final assembly operators themselves. Within one week, the audit defects dropped to nearly zero, the customer defects also dropped to nearly zero, and customer satisfaction began to improve immediately. We were out on the shop floor one evening during the second shift when a team leader shut down the final assembly line because one of the machines (a staking machine) was producing defects on about every third part. Only a few weeks before, the product would have been allowed to pass through. In this way, the defect was caught at its source. The general manager of the facility called the team out into the center of the assembly area and publicly congratulated the members for catching the defect and taking corrective action. The news of this event spread throughout the plant within a few hours, helping philosophy to change throughout the company. No one ever looked back. Customer rejects plummeted.

We also remember a similar story we learned while talking to a 25-year veteran machinist. The company for whom he worked also had eliminated the quality inspection function, and given the responsibility to the operators. One of us asked the question, "How many bad parts did you make today?" The answer was quick, "Not a one." He showed us the statistical process control data on his machine that ensured he was producing parts within specifications. When asked how he liked the new system he said, "I haven't enjoyed coming to work so much in all my 25 years here. You know, there's no one lookin' over my shoulder. I'm responsible for quality—no one else."

Here is a case that illustrates the myopic view sometimes held by management. One of us had just taken responsibility for a new plant that was very traditional in its approach to manufacturing. During a plant review, the question was raised about giving the shop-floor operators responsibility for their own quality. The question sparked a 45 minute debate about whether this was a good idea because productivity would suffer and customer shipments would be jeopardized. The plant's management team had missed the entire point. They actually felt that it was okay to ship substandard parts to the customer as long as the delivery schedule was met. Needless to say, a change in philosophy was needed.

Making all plant personnel responsible for their own quality sounds simple, and it is. Most importantly, it works.

## The Concept of Self-Stop

In the Toyota System, all automated processes are designed to detect defects at their source of manufacture and to stop the production process immediately so that the source of the defect can be determined and corrected.

We have seen this philosophy implemented in different ways. In the purist application, it means shutting down production for the process where the defect is detected. For example, the stamping presses for producing automotive body panels usually have sensors to detect the proper positioning of the sheet steel and the two halves of the stamping die. If the alignment is not perfect, the press stops and sounds an alarm. This practice is critical from safety, quality, and investment perspectives. If the press closes on a misaligned die, severe damage will be done to the die and the press. More importantly, operators in the vicinity of the press could be injured.

In other cases, automatic equipment or in-process inspection stations will detect a defect and remove it from the process. In

160

more sophisticated applications of this approach, the defective parts will be categorized and automatically be deposited into a bin for a given class of defect (i.e. an automatic Pareto analysis that identifies the most frequent defects). Purists may say that this approach does not meet Toyota's standards. When making the transformation, it is often a necessary transitional phase. Defects are detected at their source and removed from the process, but production of good parts continues. Subsequent actions separate the lean company from a traditional one. In a lean company, the defects will be analyzed and corrective action will be taken to eliminate the cause(s) of the defects. (We will discuss root-cause problem solving later.) In a traditional company, the defect data will often be collected, tabulated, sorted, graphed, but nothing will be done to correct the problem. The data will disappear into the computers of the Quality Department, never to be seen again until someone happens to ask for it. When data is available and distributed to the organization, it refers to issues that occurred 2 to 3 months before. Actions that might have been taken may not be relevant to the current situation. People may not remember the specific set of circumstances, and may not repeat them precisely in the same manner.

The concept of self-stop applies to rework processes as well. Whenever rework exists, a process is not in control. To achieve six sigma quality, rework must be systematically eliminated. Even at Toyota, however, some rework exists on an ongoing basis. As was discussed in Part I of this book, at the end of the vehicle assembly line are a fixed number of rework bays (usually about 10) used to correct any final defects. When they become filled, management knows something is wrong. The assembly line is shut down and corrective action taken.

The key is to find and eliminate defects where they happen, whether they are detected automatically, by operators, or by a combination, isn't important. Their cause must be eliminated systematically. All too often, operators see problems, and report them to management, only to get the response, "Never mind, keep going. At least we'll be able to send something to the customer."

Consider the message that attitude sends.

### Mistake Proofing (Poka Yoke)

The concept of mistake proofing (poka yoke in Japanese) is critical to achieving six sigma quality. Mistake proofing means that the product and the process are designed so that a mistake cannot occur. The connectors on a personal computer illustrate a type of mistake proofing. Try to insert the printer cable or the display cable the wrong way. You can't. The connector is shaped so that only one orientation is possible.

Here's another example. A plastic part was held in place by four pegs, two at top and two at bottom. All four pegs were the same size, so it was possible to install the part upside down. By making one of the bottom pegs larger than the others, correct assembly was assured every time.

During the design phase, engineers must ensure that parts cannot be assembled incorrectly. This is the easiest and least costly approach. Nonetheless, mistake proofing must be carried into the manufacturing process, particularly where it has not been part of the design process for products already in production.

An operator was putting an adhesive label titled "Center" onto a seat belt buckle to indicate that the buckle was to be used in the center of the back seat. The buckle did not have guide markings for the placement of the label, although a picture guide was provided in the work instructions. Not surprisingly, the label was often crooked and was not consistently placed in the same position on the buckle. Since this was a product feature that was visible to the consumer, the aesthetics of label placement were important (even though it had no effect on the actual functioning of the buckle). The solution involved creating a fixture to hold the buckle and a simple mechanical press to apply the label exactly the same way every time. Total investment was a few hundred dollars, and a major source of customer dissatisfaction was eliminated.

Mistake proofing often involves fixtures that ensure the correct orientation of the parts being assembled. Sometimes color coding is used. For example, hoses or cables can be color coded to ensure that they are always connected to the proper locations. The work instructions for a given assembly can all be color coded the same way. The dies for a given class of press can also have the same color markings.

The possibilities for mistake proofing are endless. They generally require only a bit of creativity and a small investment. Again, the key is to ensure that a mistake cannot be made. Several texts have been written on this subject. We suggest reviewing one for a plethora of ideas.

## Standardized Work

Standardized work means that a given process is done the same way every time. While this may sound trivial, it isn't. The highest quality comes from repeatable processes, be they on a machine or in assembly work. In the seat belt buckle example above, the lack of standardized work was causing a quality problem. The solution in this case was a mistake proofing device that required that the same process be followed each time.

Mistake proofing is, however, often not enough. Standardized work requires that work methods and motions be studied to determine the most efficient and repeatable methods. This is documented, and that the people involved are trained in executing the process. For example, the United Parcel Service reportedly has guidelines concerning how many steps a delivery person should take in leaving the truck, and in which hand a parcel should be held in order to maximize efficiency. This is a form of standardized work.

As an aside, we find that visual work instructions using drawings or pictures are much more effective than pure text instructions, as the example below illustrates.

**Figure 2.17**

### Written work Instruction

|  |
|---|
| • Approach door |
| • Extend right hand outward towards the handle |
| • Grasp the door handle firmly in your right hand |
| • Step slightly backwards |
| • Contract your muscles in your right arm to exert a backward force to the door |

### Visual work Instruction

### First In, First Out (FIFO) Control

FIFO control of raw materials, components, subassemblies, and finished goods is absolutely critical to quality. As with most of the lean concepts, this one is simple but is often overlooked. FIFO means that parts and assemblies are passed on to the next stage of production in exactly the order they were produced. A convenience store that loads cartons of milk from inside the refrigerator case and pushes them down a shelf to the door (from which the consumer takes the milk) is maintaining FIFO control.

If a company has FIFO control, and a defective element is found in the production process, it is easy to remove any parts or assemblies that are downstream in the process. Without FIFO control, the location of defective items cannot easily be determined. A critical element of a FIFO system is that it must be easy and natural for the people who must use it and maintain it day in and day out. Flow through racks, such as the one in Figure 2.9 on page 129, are an easy way to maintain FIFO control.

Of course, flow through racks can be expensive. Another way to execute FIFO control is with lanes on the floor that are fed from one end and pulled from another. This is shown in Figure 2.10 on page 130.

Systems that are not easy to use tend to break down over time and result in a loss of FIFO control. In many electronics factories, for example, component reels are stacked one on top of another. In order to maintain FIFO control, new inventory should be put on the bottom of the pile and the oldest inventory picked from the top (or the other way around). In most cases, the new inventory is stored on the top and picked from the top, resulting in old inventory remaining permanently on the bottom (this is a Last In, First Out system). If a bad lot of capacitors is suddenly discovered, it will not be possible to know when or where they entered the production stream. This same problem will occur for any type of stacked materials (e.g. bags of plastic resin, coils of strip steel, stacks of printed circuit boards). Time after time, we have gone into a warehouse and asked how FIFO control is maintained. The answer usually is that the materials are stacked in date-code order and that the proper storing and picking sequence is *always* maintained. A quick check of locations at random reveals that this system is not followed 75% of the time. Ask this question in your own factory. It will only take a few minutes, and you will likely be appalled at what you find.

### Root Cause Problem Solving

Another key element to building in six sigma quality is to permanently eliminate defects by identifying and eliminating the root cause of problems. Root cause problem solving skills are generally weak in traditional mass producers. So much excess inventory exists that problems can remain hidden for years. If a bad batch of components is produced, they are simply discarded, and more are produced. But this doesn't fix the underlying problem.

Toyota people refer to "The Five Why's." To get to the root cause of a problem, one needs to ask "Why?" at least five times in sequence. This is like peeling away the layers of an onion. For example, a capillary tube soldered to a bellow leaks:

- Why does it leak?

  *The welding does not seal properly.*
- Why is it that it does not seal properly?

  *There is a deposit of a material inside the capillary tube.*
- Why is there a deposit inside the capillary tube?

  *Washing of the tube did not clean it.*
- Why did the washing not clean it?

  *The detergent used was not working effectively.*
- Why did the detergent not work effectively?

  *The detergent formula was not effective on this particular type of deposit.*

One effective means of tracking and analyzing problems is to use a Four Phase chart as shown in Figure 2.18. The advantage of the Four Phase chart is that it is concise, yet complete in describing the problem and the corrective actions. Something to remember is that you can be sure you have found the root cause of a problem when you can "turn it on and off," i.e. recreate the problem at will, and then cause it to go away.

There are several texts available that describe root cause problem solving techniques in detail. Collectively, these sources cover approaches such as fish bone diagrams for segregating the possible sources of a problem, Taguchi methods and Design of Experiments (DOE), Failure Mode and Effects Analysis (FMEA), multi-vari studies to determine process variability, gauge repeatability and reproducibility, process control plans, and so on. All are important elements in achieving six sigma quality.

**Figure 2.18**

## *Four Phase Corrective Action Matrix*

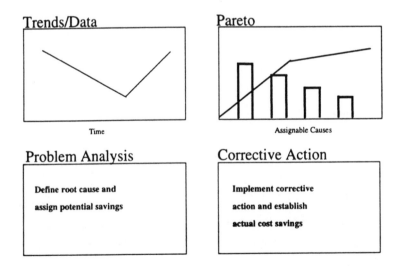

Trends/Data

Time

Pareto

Assignable Causes

Problem Analysis

Define root cause and assign potential savings

Corrective Action

Implement corrective action and establish actual cost savings

## Workforce Empowerment

A basic tenet of the lean enterprise is to push decision making to those personnel closest to a situation. Who can possibly be in a better position to recognize what needs to be done in a given situation than the one who is right there on the spot? Moreover, the lean enterprise works through empowered teams. These are teams, often comprised of individuals from various disciplines, whose job it is to address specific tasks or assignments. These teams are "empowered" because they can decide on the best course of action and take it. Individuals must shift from a mindset where supervisors told them what to do to one where the group makes decisions on everything from who will work overtime, or fill in for a worker who is out sick, to what should be done to improve output quality. They will have to think out of the box in order to determine how processes can be improved and what changes should be implemented. Perhaps as important, teams can help build an atmosphere of cooperation and esprit d'corps. For them to work properly, however, people must learn how to function as team players. It will help if they know what to expect when individuals are brought together into a unit with specific goals and objectives.

Teams typically progress through four stages. Recognizing these and anticipating the challenges they are likely to present will help ensure smooth growth and ultimate success. We'll call stage one "Forming." It is marked by uncertainty and distance between members. People in the group feel unsure about their roles and relationships. Think of it as the "becoming acquainted" part of a team's life cycle. The next stage, which is called "Norming," occurs when the team begins to settle down to become an efficient unit. Predictable patterns emerge and a style of work develops. "Storming," which happens next, is what transpires when conflicts arise. This is the critical stage, so leaders need to manage the situation and persevere. Teams often don't survive. Members may want to fold up the tent and throw in the towel rather than continue. But encourage a team to get on with it and iron out the problems they've created for themselves. Let them know that

"Storming" is normal. Let them know it's a necessary stage, and that it's the prelude to the truly productive stage that comes next. This final and fruitful stage is "Performing," when a mature team can be counted on to deliver solutions. "Performing" often is at its most spectacular in high pressure situations, on tight deadlines, or under conditions that may require superhuman effort. Top performing teams can create amazing results. Consider, for example, the team that worked to bring back safely the crew of the crippled Apollo 13 spacecraft on its ill-fated mission to the moon.

Teamwork can result in an extraordinary experience that members will never forget. The bonding that results can be very strong indeed. Even in the case of groups with modest missions, teamwork can replace apathy and discouragement with pride and enthusiasm. At the very least, members of a team that has passed through the stages we've mentioned must have learned to listen sincerely and to speak the truth, as opposed to venting and bellyaching. Caring about the success of the team and about teammates is half the battle. This can go a long way in helping people learn how to put what may be good for the group as a whole ahead of selfish motives.

A team can be almost any group that has closely linked jobs, and can cut across what would be different departments in a traditional organization. To break down the barriers, we think of team members as representatives of various disciplines rather than as having different functions. The distinction is subtle, but it helps bring down walls. Every effort should be made to keep teams consistent from one day to the next. Individuals should remain together as much as possible so that esprit d'corps can build.

It is also important to have personnel from different organizations participating on a project, as they often can see things that people who are involved in activities daily do not see. When conducting kaizen events, it may be beneficial to have participants from other parts of the company, or perhaps even from other locations.

Workers on the factory floor in a lean organization are grouped into teams of production cells. These teams meet regularly to discuss and solve problems. It is also important for group leaders, or supervisors, to be out on the floor with the people for whom they are responsible, so that it becomes clear that they are part of the team and not part of a management group that's far away in an ivory tower. To ensure this, we often reposition their desks so that they are on the production lines, rather than hidden from view in an office. This forces a leader to be attentive.

In the lean enterprise, leaders actually are there to serve. It is the leader's job to motivate and coach. The leaders' responsibility is to facilitate the work of others. Moving their desk often helps supervisors make a mental switch. But not always. Even after the move, some continue to operate in the same old way by cracking a whip. Nevertheless, they must learn to be participative, which often requires training and coaching. And the fostering of teams.

The question is often raised, "What can a top manager do or say that will get a supervisor to shift gears?"

We can think of two things. One is a stick, the other a carrot. First, the top manager can make it clear that the individual has a choice of either changing, or leaving. The carrot is a "job well done." Improved performance and goals accomplished provide the rewards that motivate, rather than the feeling of being in a position of power over others. This will work if the focus can be shifted where it belongs—to end results—to filling customer needs, to increased quality, and lower costs.

We've found that plants that perform best have meetings

between operators and leaders at the beginning of each shift. These last 10-15 minutes. The group looks at its performance from the day before, and at production goals for the day ahead. Work assignments are reviewed and any special instructions noted. Quality or production issues are reviewed. If someone on the team didn't come to work, or if someone has to leave early, this will be discussed and how to handle it resolved. Overtime schedules are reviewed and replacements determined if necessary. Whether the group is ahead or behind its production schedule is discussed. If it is behind, the group decides what can be done to catch up.

Once a week, groups also meet for half an hour to discuss performance issues. This is the forum for suggestions on how to improve. If suggestions made in previous meetings haven't been implemented, a report is made on where they stand.

Add up the time spent in meetings and you'll find that workers spend an hour and a half each week, which may seem excessive. But we've found that it pays. In one plant, unit output ranged from 42,000 to 45,000 product units each day prior to their implementation. Today, the plant averages 54,000 units a day with the same number of people. But that's not all. The plant had been producing 2,000 boxes a day, and 120 to 150 of these were rejected largely due to quality problems. Now the plant produces 2,400 boxes a day and no boxes are rejected. Rework has been substantially reduced and virtually eliminated.

When a quality problem arises in this plant, the operators involved are sent to call on the customer. Imagine what happens when a worker who has heard about a problem firsthand gets together the next day with the rest of the team. The impact is dramatic. People pay attention. Problems are taken seriously, and solutions quickly found. This is continuous pursuit of improvement in action.

In the transition to team empowerment, it is important to

celebrate successes. Most managers are quick to have a meeting to talk about what isn't going right. They are correct in doing so. But in order to provide positive reinforcement, meetings also should be held about what is going right. There should be celebrations. The head of manufacturing or the general manager, might buy coffee for the team that has scored a success. Or maybe it's a cake complete with candles. Or pizza. Everyone who had a hand in the success should be invited. But we've found that it is best to limit participation only to those actually involved. Allowing interlopers to join in can destroy the meaning, and water down the significance, of the celebration. Let the others score their own successes, and get their own free pizza and a pat on the back.

Empowered teams are a fundamental way of working throughout the lean enterprise. In a figurative sense, they help bring down walls between departments, but we've found that it can actually help to literally bring them down. In going lean, we strive for as much transparency as possible by putting everyone together where they can see one another and are encouraged to interact. For example, in many large organizations, process and design engineers do not speak to one another unless absolutely necessary, even though they are in the same building. Design Engineering develops the product and then "slips the blueprints under the door." In an organization where this is the situation, you might put all engineers on one floor with no walls whatsoever. In any case, many problems can be eliminated before they occur if design engineers are required to present their design to other disciplines, such as process engineering, quality assurance, marketing and sales, in a design review meeting at various stages in the development process. The design engineers should then consider all suggestions and report back to the group concerning the modifications made.

Teams such as these should be comprised of representatives of all areas of the business that have a stake in a product, including the customer. The team should also have representatives from finance, quality assurance, and materials supply, because the end product will benefit from the perspective of each. Products should be designed for ease of manufacturing, and this requires a clear understanding of the manufacturing process. It makes sense, therefore, for process engineering to have a seat on the team.

As the organization evolves, the role to be played by Human Resources will become increasingly important. The head of the company needs to define the culture to be attained, and Human Resources must identify changes that have to be accomplished in order to arrive at this. Human Resources also should remain attentive to developments that may throw up impediments to a lean enterprise culture. This means having a steady finger on the pulse of the company grapevine, and advising the various leaders on activities to be performed in order to ensure a successful cultural change. The transformation no doubt will require consistent and systematic training of everyone in the company.

## Visual Management/Visual Factory

A lean factory makes extensive use of visual management techniques—management by sight, not by computer. The objective is to be able to "see" the factory—its work flow, its performance, its problems, and its opportunities for improvement. Visual management is critical to achieving truly empowered employees. Empowerment is not possible without information, and the best way to ensure that information is available is through simple visual management techniques.

How many times have you seen factories where critical information (such as quality, delivery, or cost) is kept hidden by a few individuals who feel that they are the only ones with a "need to know"—as if it were a key military secret? At the same time, you ask people on the shop floor about such matters and they don't have a clue. Such an environment will never result in world class performance. By contrast, you can walk into a world class lean facility and immediately get the "feel" or "hum" of the factory. You can also walk around and see information boards that display critical information for all to see—even when the news is not good (such as a customer quality problem). These visual facilities are much more likely to produce world class results because the entire organization will have access to crucial information.

We have already discussed many visual management techniques in other sections of Part II. The entire 5S system is a critical underpinning of visual management—a safe, orderly, and immaculately clean workplace. The 5S system uses devices such as kanban squares and shadow boards to ensure a "place for everything and everything in its place."

**Figure 2.19, Shadow Board for Tool Organization**

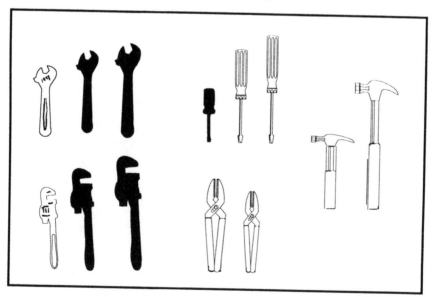

Flow-through racks and other FIFO inventory management methods provide visual information on inventory levels. The visual warehouse is organized so that all quantities of a given part number are kept in the same location. This way an operator can see what the inventory levels are. The lean factory will not use the typical "random access" warehouse techniques of most MRP systems. In random access systems, the computer assigns the storage locations for parts when they are stored. A given part number could be in several locations and only the computer knows where. How many times have you seen people scrambling to find missing parts because the information in the computer was wrong? Toyota's limitation on the number of rework bays is another visual management method. If the bays are full, the entire plant knows that something is wrong, just by looking. And, the use of andon lights to signal a call for materials or maintenance is another method of visual management.

Let's move on to some additional methods of visual management. The best visual factories are laid out so that parts "flow" from incoming receiving through to fabrication and subassembly operations and then on to final assembly. If you are

**Figure 2.20, Idealized Factory Flow**

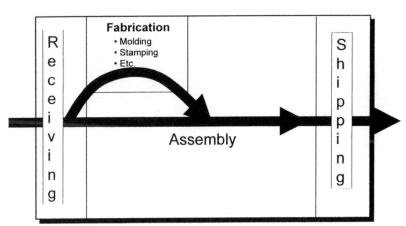

standing on a balcony in such a facility, you can almost see the flow. In fact, a floor plan showing the flow will be prominently displayed. Again in contrast, many mass production facilities look more like a labyrinth or rabbit warren with small randomly arranged rooms. Figure 2.20, to be found on the previous page, illustrates an ideal factory flow from receiving, through fabrication, on to assembly, then on to shipping. This chart is oversimplified, and most plants (unfortunately) have a combined shipping and receiving dock. If you were to start a greenfield operation, however, this is how the plant should be arranged.

Another critical item of the visual factory is information display. Information should be displayed at least two levels: (1) Individual work area performance or department performance and (2) Overall plant performance. A display board that might be used in a final assembly cell to address safety, 5S status, quality, delivery, training, and cost data. As shown below in Figure 2.21, each parameter would be tracked using a trend line, and the causes of deviations from goals are prioritized in a Pareto chart, along with corrective actions. We have seen boards like this where the information is set down manually and attached to the board

**Figure 2.21, Visual Display Board for a Work Cell**

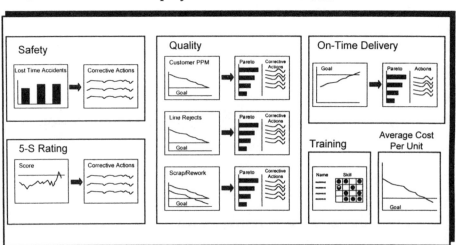

by thumbtacks. We have also seen cases where small Plexiglas holders (8 1/2" x 11" or A4 size) are fastened permanently to the board, and the sheets of paper are slipped into the holders. It really doesn't matter as long as the information is clear, legible and available for all to see.

A cell display should also include a board that describes production vs. hourly output targets (Figure 2.22) so that short-term performance can be assessed during the day. The reasons for variances, plus or minus, are accounted for in a column reserved for "remarks," or "comments." In this way a team can see where it stands in relation to the output goal for a shift, and adjust the pace of work accordingly. This also enables indirect personnel to identify problems that may be inhibiting operators. It is important to explain this board to the operators, so that they clearly understand that it has not been installed to monitor and control their performance, but rather it is there for their use, exclusively. The "comments" area permits operators to address occurrences that may require improvement.

The display boards for a fabrication department (e.g. stamping, plastic molding, die casting) might include changeover times and machine uptime, but not include delivery reliability since it will be supplying internal operations via kanban. The key

**Figure 2.22, Cell Production Status Board**

| Model | Time | Work minutes | Goal | Actual | Diff | Number of people | Comments |
|-------|------|-------------|------|--------|------|------------------|----------|
|  | 8:00 - 9:00 | 50 | 50 | 48 |  | 1 | Machine #3 down 10 min. |
|  | 9:00-10:00 | 60 | 60 | 62 | +2 | 1 |  |
|  | 10:00-11:00 | 50 |  |  |  |  |  |
|  |  |  |  |  |  |  |  |
|  |  |  |  |  |  |  |  |

is to include information that is relevant to the operation.

Displays of overall factory performance would typically include the same information as a final assembly cell, but aggregated for the entire plant. We also like to see financial information displayed. There is often sensitivity about publicly displaying profit and return-on-investment data. If this is an issue, you can display this information in the form of an index where "100" represents the budget and a graph can show deviations from budget. The overall factory communication center should also include displays on major events (e.g. customer visits) and other current events, as well as recognition in the form of customer quality awards, employee of the month, and so forth. There's no right or wrong here. The objective is to communicate enough information so that everyone in the factory is aware of key information, but at the same time, isn't overloaded with data.

When a company installs communication boards of the type discussed here, there is usually an immediate improvement in results.

## Continuous Pursuit of Perfection

The last fundamental of lean production that we will cover is the continuous pursuit of perfection—the idea that one must always strive to eliminate waste in the organization and constantly make improvements even if they are small and incremental.

The most important aspect of this fundamental is the mindset of the management and the people. It is a mindset that believes perfection must be an ongoing goal even though it can never be fully attained. Without this mindset, companies become complacent and slow.

Goal setting is a critical element of continuous improvement. Initially, management leadership needs to set goals for quality improvements, including waste reduction, lead-time reduction, etc. We have found, however, that empowered teams often set more aggressive goals than management will—and will usually achieve them. This raises a critical issue concerning management style. Positive reinforcement is important, which means celebrating successes. It is equally important *not* to punish a team if they fail to achieve an aggressive goal. Rather, management should act as coach to help the team understand what went wrong (including assessing whether the goal was too aggressive), and to enable the team to learn from the experience. This type of mutual support goes a long way toward building top-performing companies.

The systematic elimination of waste becomes a constant focus of continuous improvement efforts. This includes the waste from: (1) overproduction, (2) unnecessary conveyance of parts (3) wasted operator motion, (4) waiting, (5) quality defects/rework, (6) inventory, and (7) all other types of activity that do not add

**Figure 2.23, Inventory Hides Problems**

Inventory is like a river. As the level gets lower, boulders appear.
Reducing inventory brings problems to the surface and forces their resolution.

value to the product. Inventory is perhaps the hardest category for mass producers to accept as unnecessary waste. Traditional mass producers view inventory as a security blanket to ensure that production can continue when something goes wrong. Lean producers view inventory as a sign that the production process is not yet perfect. It is critical to continue improving everything until inventory is finally eliminated.

This brings up the subject of a system for input to facilitate continuous improvement. We've observed an ongoing debate about suggestion systems, which have been a hallmark of Japanese companies. Some suggestion programs are very successful, and others are dismal failures. The successful programs seem to have some common characteristics. First, improvement ideas should be reviewed, approved, and implemented at as low a level in the organization as possible—ideally within a team working on the shop floor or in a supporting department. This means that team leaders must have authority to approve expenditures up to a certain level. The "right sized" parts washer that was discussed earlier in the section on JIT production is an example. It cost a couple of hundred dollars and was approved by the cell's team leader. It was implemented within a few days with very little paperwork or effort needed to move it through a bureaucracy.

Second, it is critical to ensure that teams set aside time each day to discuss improvement ideas. The third element relates to suggestions for improvements outside one's immediate work area. In this case, most companies will have a suggestion box for the submission of ideas. The successful programs will have a bias for quick evaluation and implementation, i.e., there must be a good reason for rejecting an idea and that reason must always be communicated back to the person who suggested it. Our Toyota colleagues tell us that about 90% of all ideas are implemented, with constant feedback on the status of implementation.

A fourth characteristic is a recognition system. Most successful companies will have some form of reward program for the best ideas. Usually, an annual or semi-annual recognition event is held with nominal prizes awarded and lots of peer attention. Sometimes, there is a monetary reward (e.g. a percentage of savings). We have found, however, that monetary programs often don't work and become excessively bureaucratic.

It is common for suggestions to require assistance from other departments in a factory. For example, process changes sometimes require process engineering to design new fixtures or modifications to equipment. The leadership team in the factory must prioritize these programs. Communication of these priorities is important so that people who suggest ideas are not discouraged if they have to wait a while.

Another common issue is design changes. We have found many instances where improvements require that design engineering make a modification to a specification or drawing— usually because a thorough analysis of design-for-manufacturability was never done. We recall one instance when an operator was spending a tremendous amount of time forming the leads of an integrated circuit so that they would fit in the holes on the printed circuit board. It turned out that design engineer had laid out the PC board incorrectly. The problem had existed for about six months, but no one had done anything about it. It wasn't corrected until the operator was given an opportunity to suggest the improvement. Once the issue was brought to the attention of the design engineer, it was fixed.

Here again is a strong need for management leadership. We have seen situations where Engineering or another function is "too busy" to fix a production problem they caused in the first place. Plant management or the general manager must ensure that such an attitude is not tolerated.

## Key Points and Highlights

In Part II, we've attempted to provide some detail on transforming a traditional mass production factory into one that is lean. The discussion centers around six fundamental principles of lean production.

1. The workplace is safe, orderly, and immaculately clean.

2. Products are built just in time, and only to customer demand.

3. Six sigma quality is built into the product and the process.

4. Empowered work teams make key decisions on the shop floor and in supporting functions.

5. Visual management techniques are used to spread critical information throughout the factory.

6. There is a relentless pursuit of perfection.

We believe that individuals who understand these basic principles of the lean factory will tend to make the right decisions in implementing lean programs. They will also be able to determine their mistakes and be self-correcting, i.e., if a given program is not working right, the team will recognize it and take another path.

The lean transformation generally begins on the shop floor in final assembly and expands from there. The work area is cleaned and organized using the 5S approach. Process-mapping techniques are used to change the current batch process to a continuous-flow process. A kanban system is installed to link customer demand to final assembly, and then from final assembly to internal and external suppliers. The responsibility for quality is transferred to the final assembly team and they are trained in six sigma quality techniques that include statistical process control, root-cause problem solving, and mistake proofing methods. The teams also receive empowerment training so that they can transition from a "command and control" management approach to self-managed work teams. Visual display boards are installed to disseminate key information to all team members, and a culture/practice of continuous improvement is established. Once these actions have been accomplished for part of the factory, it is time to start over again, and again and again, until the entire factory is transformed.

This is the essence of the shop floor process. It should not take more than 6 to18 months to transform a moderate sized facility. Significant resistance to the change is likely to develop, especially from concrete heads who will likely be required to leave the company. Be prepared for a backlash and ensure everyone knows that turning back from the lean journey is not an option. Keep at it because the rewards are worth it.

Now we will move on to Part III, which discusses expanding the lean program from the shop floor to the rest of the enterprise.

# PART III

# Spreading Lean Throughout the Company

A lean factory alone does not make a lean enterprise. It is necessary to extend shop floor fundamentals to the entire company, and eventually to expand this outward to customers and suppliers—essentially to the entire value chain. Our intention in Part III is to introduce the subject of the lean enterprise and provide a "20,000 foot" overview. (We expect to expand on the subject in a subsequent edition of *Lean Transformation.)*

The philosophy behind the concepts introduced here is that the factory floor is the core of any manufacturing company, i.e., the company does not make any money until a product is shipped out of the plant. Sounds obvious, but think of how many companies where this is not the case. Many are primarily centered around engineering or marketing, often neglecting the factory in the big picture. In this world, the factory is a necessary evil—"After all, we have to make our technological wonders somewhere, don't we?" In a lean enterprise, there is a strong balance among the key functions. It is recognized that unless a quality product can be produced at a competitive cost the company is not going to do very well. And, while we've focused these comments on manufacturing companies, the same can be true for service companies.

We will begin the discussion by talking about the functions that support manufacturing, followed by the role of Sales/Marketing in expanding lean concepts to the customer, and the role of Purchasing/Supplier Quality Assurance in expanding them to suppliers. Then we'll touch on lean management structures.

## Design Engineering

Design Engineering is critical to a successful lean transformation. The function must do two things extremely well. First, it must be capable of designing and introducing new products in a very short period of time—less than 6 months for electronic products and no more than 6-9 months for products requiring major tooling. Second, it must ensure that its products can be manufactured efficiently. Unfortunately, both attributes are rare, especially in traditional mass manufacturing companies. We've seen many companies where, even though Design Engineering is in the same building as the factory, they might as well be a thousand miles away. The engineers never go onto the shop floor, minimal concern exists for design for manufacturability (DFM), and engineering management could not care less. They're too busy "focusing on the future."

Since we are both ex design engineers, we understand this focus. We felt the same way early in our careers. For Henderson, an awakening occurred when he was put in charge of manufacturing an electronic system for which he had been the lead design engineer. His team couldn't build the system and couldn't test it. A miserable six months of redesign ensued, but a valuable lesson was learned.

A critical attribute of a successful Design Engineering function is the mindset that says "manufacturing is crucial to the success of the company, and I have to take a lead role to ensure that my designs can be produced at six sigma quality levels, and at a competitive cost."

### Design for Manufacturability (DFM)

Let's assume for the moment that Design Engineering is working on the right product for the market with the right timing. (We'll discuss Marketing's role later.) DFM then becomes a critical element of the design process. Various methods can ensure DFM, some complex and some simple. Common to all is that the product and the manufacturing process are designed simultaneously.

Most Computer Aided Design (CAD) systems include software for mechanical or electronic tolerance-stack-up analyses. These are statistical programs used to ensure that the product will function when all the expected process and component variations are stacked on top of each other. An example might be the design of a plastic gear cluster that drives a timing sequence. The expected variation of each gear will affect the performance of the entire cluster. The accuracy requirement will drive the selection of materials and process parameters.

CAD systems also can provide process simulation information such as mold flow analysis for designing the tooling for plastic parts. The mold flow program will simulate the plastic flow in the mold to help determine where gates should be placed and the proper dimensioning of resin flow paths. In other cases, the manufacturing rules can be stored inside the CAD system. This is especially true for the layout of electronic printed circuit boards where the CAD system can be programmed to ensure that components are oriented in an optimal manner for automatic insertion machines, and are not placed too close together. In one company we visited, the designers were not using this feature of the CAD system even though it was available because it "stifled their creativity." This company had terrible product launch problems, and usually ended up reworking the circuit board layout after it was in production This should not have been a big surprise.

Design engineers must build mistake-proofing into the product wherever possible. For example, if two mating parts should only be inserted in a single orientation, the connecting devices should be configured to ensure that incorrect assembly is impossible. A way to ensure adequate mistake proofing is to have assembly workers build early prototypes of the product, using a mock-up of the final assembly line. The improvement ideas will flow freely at a stage in the design process when it is easy to make changes.

It is important for design engineers to have actual manufacturing experience and process knowledge. When this is the case, simultaneous product and process engineering occurs easily. It remains baffling to us that many design engineers have very little practical knowledge of the processes for which they are designing. When this is the case, it is incumbent upon them to go onto the shop floor to seek advice and input from those who do know. As one remedy, many organizations will include manufacturing engineers on the design team. When the resources are available, this is an excellent way to get real-time manufacturing input.

Formal design reviews are another way to help ensure DFM. Manufacturability will be critiqued, and suggestions for improvements made. Unfortunately, we've observed that formal DFM reviews are generally a poor substitute for real-time input from manufacturing. Reviews often occur too late in the process for changes to be easily made, and they are usually dominated by design engineers who are merely "punching the ticket" in a design process that mandates such a review.

### Be Reasonable about Critical Parameters

How many times have you seen a product drawing where nearly all the dimensions or other attributes are "critical" to the product? To be sure, some attributes are critical, but we have seen drawings where 20 or 30 parameters are considered so on a given part. This generally is an indication of poor design process analysis. What many engineers fail to realize is that each attribute defined as "critical" must be checked during the manufacturing process or during incoming inspection for purchased components. We have recommended on a number of occasions that these engineers and their managers spend time on the shop floor trying to maintain the flow of the process in the wake of checking this many parameters. Usually, a dramatic change occurs in what is considered critical.

### Knowledge of Logistics and the Need for Standardization

Every single component part in a factory must be ordered, received, inspected (either in the factory or by the supplier), stored, moved, and finally put into the final product. The more parts, the more complicated and expensive this process becomes, resulting in bigger warehouses, bigger computer systems, more people to receive and move parts, higher piece-part costs due to lower volumes of each individual item.

Design engineers must be knowledgeable about logistics, especially as it relates to non-standard components and long-lead items. Henderson remembers standing in the incoming staging area of one of his factories and wondering why there were 30 different varieties of engineered fasteners, each with a 12-14 week lead time. Many of the fasteners had the same diameter and thread pitch, but differed by only one or two in the total number of threads. Engineering's answer was that these dimensions were agreed to by the customer, and were critical to the functioning of the end product. A small amount of analysis showed that this conjecture was ridiculous. Customers didn't care as long as the fasteners did not exceed a maximum length (well within the varieties specified). They agreed to the change once they were made aware. Thirty varieties were reduced to six, thereby reducing warehouse space and making the ordering of parts significantly easier.

For electronic equipment manufacturers, the masked micro-processor can cause the equivalent of the fastener problem. A masked micro has its binary program "masked in" as part of the semiconductor manufacturing process. Changing a single computer instruction results in a unique part number that must be ordered

12-20 weeks in advance. It is not unusual to have unique masked micros for each individual customer application, yielding a logistical nightmare if any volatility to customer demand is present. Because of the long lead-time, the parts must be ordered using a forecast rather than the kanban system. The material planner must predict the precise customer mix 12 to 20 weeks in the future. Since this is nearly impossible, the planner will carry extra inventory, which ties up floor space and working capital, and increases obsolescence risk. One $100 million sales company with which we are familiar recently wrote off $4 million in obsolete electronics inventory—nearly a year's profit. For this reason, many companies now are changing to programmable microprocessors. The piece price is higher, but total cost per unit can be lower.

Our experience is that most design engineers will strive for standardization and simplified logistics once they understand the problem caused by parts proliferation. Those who do not, won't survive long in a lean culture.

### Driving New Product Design from Marketplace Needs

Have you ever seen an organization where the new product design priorities are established introspectively by Engineering, rather than by finding out what the customer really wants? Consider the following real life example. Engineering designed a new controller device with ten new functions never seen before in the marketplace. The head of the design team commented, "You know what? The customer picked a competitor's product that had only four new functions that was much cheaper. See, I told you they only buy on price!"

The reality of the situation was that the customer did not want the six extra features, and was unwilling to pay for them. Several months of design effort was wasted on a product that was dead on arrival. The customer's voice obviously had not been heard in the early stages. Lean companies, on the other hand, systematically include the customer in new product decisions, either through Sales and Marketing, or by direct communication with the customer. This is basic to success.

**Shortening the Design Process**

Lean companies turn out new products about every 6-9 months. How? Several methods exist, each of which could be the subject of a book. We'd like to touch on them.

The first is to develop two or more product versions in parallel, but phased about six months apart. This is how computer companies and semiconductor companies introduce new products so quickly. It may appear to be expensive, but lean companies generally spend less on manufacturing and so can afford to spend more on new product development than mass producers.

Second is the extensive use of modular designs. Lego blocks, the small, brightly-colored plastic blocks that children (and some parents) love to play with, provide a way to think of this. Give a youngster a pile of different building blocks. Before you know it, he or she will build a house, a bridge, a helicopter, or a car—all from the same basic materials. Clever engineering of a limited number of mechanical or electronic modules or a combination of the two can result in hundreds of product variations with little extra burden on the factory or logistics system.

Third is to thoroughly review the product development process and eliminate unnecessary steps. This is analogous to instituting continuous flow on the shop floor. First, map the design process as it is. Then take out unnecessary steps. Then redesign the process. The result will be crucial time savings.

Another way to speed things up is to take time out of the

tooling process. Most North American and European toolmakers require 16 to 26 weeks for a new injection mold or progressive stamping die. We recently found Asian sources that produce high quality tooling in 6 to 8 weeks. They have re-engineered their processes to take out time.

This list could go on. Let it be sufficient to say that however it is accomplished, Design Engineering must be fast, and must produce high quality, manufacturable designs. This may sound like "motherhood and apple pie," but it is an important factor separating world class companies from also-rans.

## Process Engineering

In most mass producers, Process Engineering (also known as Industrial Engineering, or Manufacturing Engineering) will focus on individual machines in an effort to get as much production out of them as possible. You might say the focus is on pieces of equipment, rather than on "total manufacturing." Typically, this means that if a machine will produce a large number of parts in a short period of time, then it will be used to make those parts even though a bottleneck exists somewhere downstream. Inevitably, the parts which have been made pile up because they have no place to go. Inventory is built, which is part of the batch and queue mentality. We've seen situations where operators of a single machine work under incentive programs that encourage them to make as many parts as possible. The quality level of the parts doesn't matter. Quality is not the goal. It doesn't matter that they can't be assembled into anything because of bottlenecks. The goal is to make as many as possible.

Process Engineering in a lean company must focus on optimizing the *flow* of products. The objective is to move everything from start to finish in a continuous flow while optimizing the process. This means removing bottlenecks. Everything should "flow like a river." We've found that once process engineers make this transition, they tend to like it. Unfortunately, some don't or won't make the transition.

We'd like to relate a story that illustrates the point about designing for flow. A few years ago, we visited a high volume electronics plant. The facility was very modern and had four state-of-the-art surface mount technology (SMT) assembly lines. SMT lines are comprised of ultra high-speed machines that place tiny electronic components (e.g. resistors, capacitors, transistors, and integrated circuits) on the surface of printed circuit boards. These machines could place up to 30,000 components per hour. The process had tremendous potential for flow manufacturing. A bare printed circuit board (PCB) was introduced at the front of the line. All components were then placed and soldered on the PCB. The board was tested, then assembled into a plastic housing with some connectors, wiring harnesses and other components. The final assembly then went through a functional test, and was ready for shipment to the customer.

The facility was, however, filled with inventory. There were batches of printed circuit boards ready to go into the SMT lines, batches of finished boards ready to go into the circuit testers, batches of tested boards ready for assembly into the final package, and (you guessed it) batches of boards ready for final functional test. There was also inventory of finished product ready to go to shipping. What was wrong with this picture? Process Engineering, with the support of plant management, had taken a continuous flow process and designed it with a batch and queue mentality.

The story continues downhill. In order to schedule the expensive SMT machines for maximum use, an elaborate MRP system was used. Since the customer schedules were constantly changing, however, it was difficult for the MRP system to keep up—wreaking havoc on the assembly floor. The throughput time was 6-7 days for a part with less than 15 minutes of touch time. The changeover time from one part to another was approximately 1.5 hours, which was built into the MRP system as a fixed, never-to-change characteristic of the process.

We asked the plant management to propose a way to reduce inventory and achieve faster throughput time. What did he come up with? A bigger and faster computer, larger batches, and even more finished goods inventory in order to deal with the customer demand volatility. The story might be funny if it were not true.

Let's look at the lean solution that was finally implemented after new management was brought in. One of the process engineers and a technician were asked what it would take to reduce changeover time to less than 10 minutes. The process engineer described all the obstacles in the way. The technician thought for a moment and said, "Gee, no one ever asked me that before." Then he said, "First I would need all the component reels on the machine for all the board combinations of boards we have to make. Then, I'd need more memory in the SMT machines so we could store all the assembly programs on line. We'd also need to make some modifications to the transport rails for the PCBs so that they could adjust to different widths automatically." Within 15 minutes, the technician had laid out most of the solution to the problem. The added investment per machine wasn't cheap. (It was about $25,000 each for memory and component reels.) But it was a good investment when measured against the previous downtime cost in changeover time of a $750,000 line.

Eventually, the process engineer caught on. He figured out that by assigning certain PCB groupings to each of the four lines, the combination of component reels required for each line could be reduced (as well as the extra memory requirement). He concluded that a 10-minute changeover time not only could be achieved, it could be beaten.

The happy ending is that the team was able to reduce changeover time to about 10 seconds by adding a bar code to each PCB panel (a panel held about 6-12 individual PCBs), and by having the machine read the code and dynamically reprogram itself for each panel. Economic lot size now was one panel. All the processes then were put into continuous flow, and throughput time was reduced to 20 minutes, which was little more than the touch time of each board. By adding a kanban pull system, the factory was also able to eliminate nearly all its finished goods inventory and still accommodate customer volatility. The hulking computer was downsized. The inventory reduction was approximately $1 million—not a bad return on a $100,000 investment. Also, quality defects plummeted since problems were identified almost immediately, instead of weeks after a given subassembly had been produced.

The point of this case history is that process engineers need to think about flow, to consider flow the end objective to be achieved, and not worry so much about the output of individual machines.

Here's another example of narrow focus. This time the problem was minimizing labor hours instead of focusing on overall productivity. The final assembly of a line for an electromechanical control had four final test machines, each doing the same operation. One worker operated two machines. Engineers had been trying to find ways to increase labor productivity and had spent a good deal of time and effort analyzing operator movements. They'd calculated everything to the fraction of a second, but even so, it was impossible to produce more than 120 units an hour. Upon looking at the situation differently, however, it became apparent that the test machines were not being used to maximum capacity. The solution was to redistribute the work by putting one operator on each of the four test machines (essentially adding twice as much labor in the final test process). The net result was 300 units produced per hour, more than double the 120 figure. But there was something even more important. The same equipment now produced twice as much product, which meant output could be doubled without capital outlay. This plant had 30 sets of equipment. Half of it was no longer needed and could be used in other locations, or it could be sold. Thus, return on capital investment was doubled.

Why didn't the process engineers see this? Because they had been doing things the same way for so long they had stopped questioning why things were done as they were. We're reminded of a story about the woman who was showing her daughter how to cook a leg of lamb. She explained what ingredients were used such as garlic and parsley and other spices. She got out her baking pan, put the leg of lamb on the counter, took a knife, and said, "You begin by cutting the leg here." She started cutting just above the ankle. It wasn't easy.

"Why, Mother? Why do you cut the leg?" the daughter asked.

The mother stopped. She looked at the leg. Then her eyes met the daughter's. "To tell the truth, I don't know. It's the way my mother did it."

"Let's give grandma a call," the daughter said.

They soon had her on the line.

"Grandma," the daughter said. "Mom's telling to me how to cook leg of lamb, and I've got a question. Why do you cut the leg?"

"Oh!" The grandmother laughed out loud. "Because my pan isn't long enough."

The mother had assumed that cutting the leg was a necessary step. If the daughter hadn't asked *why*, she and future generations might still be expending energy on an activity that added no value.

### Right Sizing of Equipment

An additional key change that process engineers need to make is to stop thinking about huge batch-oriented equipment and to focus instead on "right sized" pieces of equipment that can be put into the flow of the process. The aircraft carrier size heat treating oven can be replaced with smaller in-line machines. Large wave soldering machines get replaced with new "desk top" models. The mammoth batch parts washer may be replaced with a small in-line "car wash" type washer. And so on.

In almost all cases, a lean producer will have about 30-40% less investment in automation than a mass producer. "Monolith" sized batch processing equipment can disappear, conveyors that merely move parts may be significantly reduced, complex robotics often can be replaced with simple, and mistake-proofed manual processes.

In summary, it is Process Engineering's responsibility to translate customer takt time into continuous flow processes. This means balancing assembly lines to achieve continuous flow that match customer demand, which may or may not require the optimization of individual machines. Process engineers also need to focus on finding material handling solutions in order to ensure uninterrupted flow.

## Quality Assurance

In Part II, we discussed the subject of "Building quality in the product and the process." For the lean producer, the Quality Assurance (QA) function is the "spiritual leader" behind this concept. QA concentrates on quality *assurance*, not on quality *inspection*. In traditional factories, if someone on the shop floor is asked who is responsible for quality, the answer will likely be, "Our quality inspector." Ask the same question in a lean factory. The operators will invariably say *they themselves* are responsible.

They personalize whatever they do, and so it becomes each individual's responsibility to produce products without defects. The result is that the number of quality inspectors can be reduced to virtually zero. They aren't needed because every employee is an "inspector." Everyone looks out for defects, and calls attention to them when they appear. Similarly, design engineers and process engineers will take ownership of quality.

What, then, is the focus of QA in a lean organization? A key responsibility is to set up systems that help ensure quality, e.g. which parts require incoming inspection, how component lot tracing will be carried out, ensuring that FIFO material flow is designed into the process, working with design engineers to ensure that mistake proofing is built into the products, working with Process Engineering to ensure that QA procedures are built into the assembly lines.

QA personnel also need to become highly skilled problem solvers. When a conversion to continuous flow manufacturing takes place, serious quality defect issues usually surface almost immediately. The problems existed all along, but were hidden by inventory. Solving these should be a team effort. Nevertheless, particular technical expertise (including statistical capability, engineering capability, and so on) often is required. QA personnel need to be highly skilled in "root cause problem solving" techniques as well as other specialized methods. At Henderson's company, Invensys, these individuals are trained in six sigma problem solving methodologies and are called "Master Black Belts," "Black Belts," or "Green Belts," according to their level of training and skill. They work internally within their organizations and also with customers and suppliers. It is part of the lean enterprise culture that whenever a quality problem exists, it needs to be fixed. The most serious problems are taken first. Then the black belt works his or her way down to the next.

QA will also take the lead in analyzing defective parts that are returned from the customer. Each defect must be logged and tracked as the root cause problem of the defect is analyzed. Here is where lot tracing systems are crucial.

Defective products that are returned by customers must be analyzed carefully along with the process or system that created them. One obstacle to this can be that a defective product may be four or five weeks old by the time it is returned. It must then be traced to the shift and cell that was responsible. So, a tracking system (lot tracing) must be put in place that will allow the determination of the date the product was made as well as the line or cell that made it.

In addition, when a defect is found, information must flow quickly to those who can do something about it. To facilitate this, it may be helpful for QA to map how this process is now handled.

The highest possible quality is absolutely a top priority in the lean enterprise. Under the "Workforce Empowerment" heading, we discussed how production teams need to meet daily to review the previous day's quality performance. Under "Visual Management" we described displays that workers maintain to document quality problem occurrences. A production line, for example, needs to stop whenever a quality issue arises. If this is a nonnegotiable rule, the pressure will be on to solve recurring problems. Such a stoppage can be triggered automatically by a quality control measuring device, or an individual operator can stop the line by pulling a lever. Sometimes different color lights are used as signals. If the light is green, everything is working fine. Yellow may be a warning that a problem is looming—for example, that materials are needed. Red usually means a problem has occurred and everyone should stop.

If a good system is in place, and it can be assured that the process is stable and will remain so, the lean enterprise and its customers will be able to count on receiving products that are virtually defect free.

### Metrology Lab and Gauge R&R

An additional responsibility of QA is to maintain the laboratories for measurement equipment and test equipment. QA must also establish standards and tracking for "gauge repeatability and reliability." This is a system to routinely check measurement gauges on the shop floor (and elsewhere in the company) to ensure that they are functioning correctly. Without such a system, it's likely that erroneous quality readings will be taken during the production process, resulting in defective products.

One very simple system we've seen in use is a visual indicator telling the "owner" of the gauge that it is time to have it checked. The indicator is a color-coded sticker that has a month and a year on it. At the end of the month indicated, the gauge must be checked to see if it is still in calibration. QA also retains a log of every piece of equipment that has a sticker in order to see which items are overdue. This double check system, properly maintained, will ensure that gauges and instruments are always in top condition.

## Finance

The Finance function plays a major role in the lean transformation, and can be a tremendous catalyst, or a major inhibitor, to the process.

### The Problem with Standard Cost Systems

Traditional cost accounting processes are generally not lean, either in theory or in practice. Most involve standard costing systems that may look good on paper, but rarely provide an accurate measure of actual product cost.

Traditional standard cost systems, and many activity-based systems, draw careful distinctions between direct and so-called indirect labor costs. Vast overhead pools or complicated driver mechanisms are devised to accumulate and spread these indirect costs over the supposedly "productive direct labor." From a lean enterprise standpoint, our methods demonstrate time and again that there is no meaningful difference between direct production labor and so-called indirect labor. There is also no definitive "Generally Accepted Accounting Principles" reason why there must be such a distinction. A handful of plants have abolished this distinction already, but most accountants cling to this destructive tradition.

Standard costs will usually center around the standard "direct" labor time involved in building a given product. (Direct labor is usually defined as the people actually working on the product—as compared to maintenance people or material handlers who are considered to be "indirect.") Overhead (indirect labor, depreciation, energy costs, maintenance, supplies, etc.) is lumped into large cost pools and then "absorbed" into the cost of the product according to some factor—usually the number of "standard" direct labor hours in the product. Overhead cost absorption could be done as would be any other major cost element such as the material content of the product. At the end of the month, actual costs are compared to total standard costs (defined as the sum of all products produced times their individual standard costs), and the difference is put into cost "variances." The variances are then classified by type (e.g. labor variances, material variances, usage variances, and price variances). Labor variances, for example, would be calculated by the actual labor cost for the month minus the aggregate standard labor cost for the month. This amount would then be split into two categories, an hourly rate variance and a number-of-hours-consumed variance. Does all this sound bewilderingly complicated? It is, unless perhaps you are an accountant. Both of us nearly flunked this portion of accounting in business school.

In spite of this effort, by the way, one still doesn't really know what it cost to produce a given product. And, as we will see later in this section, standard cost analyses can lead to disastrous conclusions. Cost variances are rarely assigned back to the products that caused them. At the end of the month what exists are the accumulated standard cost and a bunch of variances. But we really don't know how much it cost to make Product A or Product B. So what good is it? In the aggregate, your accounting records should "tie out," but you are missing critical information about the business.

Standard costing can also lead to erroneous conclusions. We saw one example where a remote control device was made on two separate assembly lines. One line was a sophisticated robotic line that cost $3.5 million, and had very low direct labor. The second line was a continuous-flow manual line with very limited automation, but much more direct labor. Overhead in this factory was absorbed by a product based on the standard labor hours in the product. This cost accounting system consistently showed that products made on the manual line were much more expensive (even at the standard cost level), mostly because of the high labor content that resulted in high overhead absorption. The products made on the manual line were produced for low volume customers and commanded a premium price. Nonetheless, the accounting system calculated that the manual line was losing money because of its high costs. What was Finance's recommendation? Buy another robotic line or exit the low volume customers.

Let's look a little deeper and see why this would have been the wrong answer. It turns out that the full cost of the robotic assembly line was not being included in the cost of products made on that line. The depreciation for the $3.5 million line went into a general overhead pool for the plant and therefore was dispersed among all the plant's products. In addition, the line had about a 30% downtime, consuming a huge amount of the maintenance resources and costs of the plant. This cost, too, went into a general pool. After conducting a detailed analysis of the true costs, it became clear that the manual line was a much cheaper source of production than the robotic line. Buying another robotic line would have been exactly the wrong thing to do. We should add that, once the downtime problem was corrected, the robotic line was still more expensive when the full cost of equipment depreciation was factored in.

Standard costing can also provide a false sense of complacency. We once saw a situation recently where an assembly cell was operating at 110% of standard. Everyone from the team members up through Process Engineering, Finance, and the plant manager thought the cell was doing great. But there was a problem. The standards included lots of rework and long changeover times for the cell (changing from one product to another). In creating the standards, Process Engineering and Finance had focused on the labor content of individual operations instead of looking at the potential output of the cell. They had also ignored key bottlenecks in the process. The kaizen team that worked on this cell was able to double its output (without increasing labor) by eliminating the rework, eliminating the bottlenecks, and by reducing the changeover time to about 30 seconds. Suddenly, performance to the old standard did not look so good—the cell had been operating at only about 55% of its capability.

Many of our Finance and Accounting colleagues will argue that a properly implemented and maintained standard cost system will yield accurate results. This may be true, but we have never seen one. The systems are so incredibly complex and cumbersome that we have invariably seen the types of compromises discussed above.

## Lean Cost Accounting

Our purpose here isn't to provide a full treatise on lean cost accounting, but rather, to give you some ideas. To be sure, accounting systems in a manufacturing company become complex because of product costing and the legitimate need to value inventory.

One concept we are using is referred to as "throughput cost accounting." It is a direct accounting system where the actual cost of producing the product is measured every day, in real time. The basic concept is to establish the hourly rate of operating a work cell or fabrication department, using a simplified activity based costing system. For example, the cost of a final assembly cell includes the people working in the cell (direct and indirect labor), the depreciation of the equipment in the cell, maintenance costs of the cell, a square-foot based cost for the space the cell occupies, and so on. The hourly cost is then the [total cost per day] divided by [the number of hours the cell operates per day]. In a cell where the number of people fluctuates, the cost per hour is adjusted throughout the day. This defines the hourly "conversion cost" of products running through this cell, i.e., the cost of converting raw materials and subassemblies into the finished product for that cell. The total conversion cost for a given run of products would then be: [the hourly cost of running the cell] times [the number of hours the cell runs for a given product] divided by [the number of parts produced]. Let's take an example. Say that an assembly cell costs $600 per hour to operate, a given run of a product is one-half hour, and 60 parts are produced. The conversion cost is then

[$600] x [0.5] / [60] = $5 per unit. Suppose there is $50 of materials cost in the product and the cell created $0.25 of scrap during the run. The total cost of the product would then be $55.25 (Materials + Conversion Cost + Scrap).

The system is simple and quite accurate.

The question obviously arises about how to handle the situation where a cell goes down during the middle of a product run. Is the hourly cost during that period charged to the product, or to overhead (later to be reabsorbed throughout the plant). The answer to this question probably depends on the situation in the plant itself. If the cell is making a very narrow range of product, it might make sense to charge downtime to the product rather than to overhead. If the cell is making a wide range of product, you may want to charge it to overhead rather than burdening an individual product that was unlucky enough to be run when the cell went down.

## Refocusing Financial Measurement Systems

To be sure, most traditional financial measurements are equally valid in a lean producer as in a mass producer. We still make full use of the P&L statement and balance sheet, and use measures such as return on sales, return on investment, cash flow, and so forth. Nonetheless, some measurements in a mass production system do not add value in the lean environment. Finance must take the lead role in eliminating non value-added measurements and in ensuring that remaining measurements provide an accurate picture of the operations.

Direct labor productivity (versus standard labor hours) (DLP) is a key measure that is reviewed with great scrutiny in many companies. We believe that reliance on this measure is misplaced. We've already seen that standard costing systems can be unreliable as indicators of true cost. DLP has a number of problems. First, the measure does not take indirect labor into account, which can be a substantial portion of labor cost. Second, standards are set on the labor content of individual operations, not on the total output potential of a work cell or other operation. Third, we have found that some companies set the standards at a level above the actual direct labor hours in order to provide stretch goals to workers. ("We must work harder—we are not achieving the standards.") This use of standards breeds frustration and cynicism in the organization, especially in union environments.

The focus on DLP can also result in some strange attitudes. One of our colleagues relates the following story. A German Meister (supervisor) in a molding shop proudly told our colleague that no productivity improvement was possible in his shop section. There was no need for him to waste time trying to implement lean techniques because there was no labor in the shop. Curious to know what the two busy ladies in the shop were doing (if it wasn't labor), our colleague asked the Meister, "What's that? Looks like labor to me."

"No, no. That's not labor," the Meister replied. "These ladies are material handlers. They're feeding the automatic production machines." According to his accounting definition they were "indirect," and shouldn't be counted in the cost of production.

Uh-huh. Yeah, right.

Here is another example of problems with DLP. One plant we know about in Maine converted its production processes to lean. Cycle time for production from start to finish fell from 120 days to only two. Customer lead times fell dramatically, as did inventory. Indirect labor was reduced as line operators took over many of the tasks formerly performed by the indirect supervisors, planners, material handling people, and QA people. Quality levels skyrocketed. The dramatic turnaround changed what had been a loss situation into a profitable plant.

Division management, however, continued to view the plant from the traditional standard cost accounting measurements, which told them that direct labor now stood at 58% efficiency. The plant manager was "called on the carpet" by the division manager, who demanded an immediate return to the old productivity levels. Meanwhile, the sister plant in France was achieving a 110% direct labor efficiency level. The burning question was, why couldn't the lean plant do likewise, if lean enterprise was so terrific? The plant manager received no help from division financial management in explaining the discrepancy, which boiled down to comparing apples to oranges. Indirect labor and inventory had fallen. Cash and book profits had improved significantly. Even so, the plant manager was fired. Later, the division manager was fired, too, when his blunder was realized. Unfortunately, the damage had been done.

At a plant in Australia, the introduction of continuous flow produced significant increases in throughput on a line that made a ten-year-old product. The conversion to single piece, continuous flow dramatically reduced both indirect and direct labor. But the new flow did not fit the old standard cost structure. None of the activities matched the previous routings. Believe it or not, the industrial engineers and the plant accountant had employees change the cell back to the batch method in order to stop the havoc which had been caused with the costings.

When we add this all up, we conclude that DLP is a meaningless measure. A better measure is the cost of producing each group of products, and the trend lines for these. By implementing a throughput cost accounting system, meaningful and accurate real-time cost information is generated. A product line profit and loss statement now has value. By tracking the cost trend lines of individual products, or groups of products, a much better sense of the productivity of the facility is obtained.

Machine utilization is another classic measure of the mass production facility driven by the mentality that says that these big mass production machines are expensive and must be used all the time, regardless of the quality levels of the parts they put out, and regardless of whether the parts are needed. In reality, machine utilization becomes another meaningless measure for performance evaluation since one should not want a machine producing parts unless a kanban has arrived requesting parts for the next down-stream operation.

Machine utilization is, however, useful for capacity planning. By knowing how much time is available, capacity planners can determine when investment may have to be added.

Another useful measure is unscheduled machine downtime. This is time that the machine was not available for production because of a breakdown. The goal in a lean facility is to eliminate all unscheduled downtime through preventive maintenance.

One measure we like to see added is *Variable Contribution Margin (VCM)*. VCM is sales minus variable costs [Sales—(Materials + Variable Labor + Scrap/Rework + Variable Overhead)]. It is a measure that is equally valid in a mass producer or a lean producer. VCM tells a company how much profit contribution each product line is making to the fixed cost of the enterprise. It also is used to predict the company's changes in profit due to short-term volume fluctuations. Full cost is certainly necessary for product pricing and for understanding the total financial health of the business. We have seen an ongoing debate about which is a better measure—fully allocated cost or VCM. We don't see it as a "one or the other" situation, but rather that both are very useful.

**Streamlining Financial Processes**

In many ways, financial processes are not much different than manufacturing processes. The Finance team has "customers." It has due dates, suppliers (of information), and batch processes complete with queues, muda and rework. Virtually all of the lean manufacturing concepts used on the shop floor, such as continuous flow and kanbans, can be brought to bear in service processes such as those in Finance. They can be valuable tools to improve quality, speed and performance.

We have already discussed changes to the costing system and the performance measurement system. Even if these changes are made, however, it is also then necessary to eliminate the work associated with collecting now useless data. The work will not go away unless Finance takes direct action to eliminate it. For example, Finance may collect data at each stage of production or assembly in order to gauge productivity, as discussed above. But when a factory employs continuous flow, the time a particular individual spends producing a certain number of parts no longer is an issue. If a hundred parts arrive at the end of the line, then each worker produced a hundred parts. Knowing this, and changing data collection accordingly, will save a great deal of time for all parties involved. A good deal of record keeping often can be eliminated.

The first thing to eliminate should be the tracking of Work in Process Inventory (WIP). In a mass production facility a tremendous amount of effort is expended to cost and track WIP inventory. Given that the value of WIP can be very high in these facilities, this activity may make sense. Accountants establish "count points" or other means to determine where a given batch of inventory is, and what its value is at that point.

If one thinks about a large, vertically integrated facility with a lot of fabrication activities (e.g. stamping, plastic molding, casting), the tracking of WIP can be a daunting task. In fact, it normally requires a very large computer (it's usually done as part of the MRP system), lots of transactions, and lots of full-time-equivalent people. But tracking of WIP in a lean factory is a complete waste of time. Typically, there will be one-half to one day of WIP. By the time the system records the tracking, it is out the door. More important, from a financial control point of view, WIP is irrelevant.

One might think Finance would automatically recognize this and make changes. But this isn't always so. We remember an experience several years ago when setting up a new, lean factory—straight out of the Toyota model. Continuous flow lines were established. A bar-coded kanban system was put in place. All material flow was on a first-in-first-out basis. Everything was looking good until the Finance Department came in with their plan for a complex WIP tracking system (to go with the MRP system and standard cost system, of course) and the projected capital expenditure for the hulking mainframe computer that would be required. Upon being questioned about it, Finance fell back to the first line of defense—the dreaded Accounting Standards Policy. This policy allegedly stated that both WIP tracking and standard costing were an absolute requirement. In reality, neither was mandated. The policy merely described the need for systems of control without specifying the exact method to be used. The person leading the lean charge won the battle, but only for a short period of time. When he went on to another role in the company, the simplified systems were quickly replaced with the complex ones, the hulking mainframe was installed, significant cost was added to the product for no value added, and the throughput of the factory was slowed dramatically. To this day, the company espouses a lean philosophy. The Finance function, however, is not on board either in philosophy, or in practice.

Another area for streamlining is time cards for direct labor. In one company where we worked, a hundred operators spent 15 minutes each day filling out time cards. This took 1,500 minutes, or 25 work hours, the equivalent of three full time employees. In addition, one employee had the task of reviewing and correcting errors in reporting, and then entering the data into a computer. So, the equivalent of four employees was devoted to this activity.

After continuous flow had been implemented, however, all Finance needed to know was how many people were involved and how many parts were made. Moreover, because WIP had been almost totally eliminated there was no longer a need to keep track of it. Therefore, the amount of record keeping could be reduced to practically zero, requiring only a few minutes each day on the part of one production associate.

In order to generate information that will be most helpful in managing a lean business, it is important to understand that lean manufacturing is comprised of production cells and families of cells. The key is to measure and manage by cell. The fundamental change to be made, then, is for information to be gathered and arranged so that activities and production can be viewed on a "same-cell" basis. This cell-driven information can then be integrated with non-manufacturing costs so that the business can be managed profitability by product line, product group, or family. This takes the accounting function beyond the aggregation of cost by plant, which can mask true business profitability. The specifics most certainly will vary with each business situation, but the principle of cost being managed and measured at the cell level should remain valid across the board. This will provide the information needed for line managers to make decisions that drive results.

Accounts Payable is another ripe area for improvement. We have seen $100 million companies where two or three people devote all their time to accounts payable. A good portion of this time is spent matching paper invoices with receipts. This problem actually can become worse in a lean company because the number of shipments from outside vendors will increase dramatically as lot sizes are reduced and delivery frequency increased. As a result, many lean companies will install an "evaluated receipts" system which eliminates most invoices. When materials are received, a signal is sent to the accounts payable system to pay the vendor for all good parts in the shipment. An immediate notice is also sent to the vendor for all rejected parts. The vendor is paid according to whatever terms and conditions have been agreed upon according to the purchasing agreements. For example, if a vendor is to be paid in 30 days, an entry will be made immediately into the accounts payable system, but the check or funds transfer will not occur until 30 days after the receipt of the parts. It sounds simple, and is.

One way to get started on a conversion of the financial function to lean might be to gather a group comprised of key people who are involved in the financial process, and hold a kaizen event. People from outside Finance should be brought in for their perspectives. Each step of the process then needs to be justified as to whether it adds value. Is it truly something internal and external "customers" should be willing to pay for?

When conducting this kaizen event, you will probably want to pick specific "services" such as the monthly closing, or you may wish to examine a process such as cash management. You might consider using central cash management from your regional headquarters, for example, and participating in regional cash pooling systems, where they exist. The cutting of checks and cash application might be outsourced to local banks. Local tax and VAT return preparation might also. Credit cards might be used to replace petty cash, cash advances, and even the entire credit and collections process for smaller customers. Define what is value-added, and ruthlessly cut muda.

A key area to scrutinize for revamping is the monthly process of "closing the books." In many companies this takes a week to accomplish—one-quarter of the month. Let's assume that you have implemented all the streamlining activities discussed above, plus many more that are generated by the finance teams. The process of closing the books should now be vastly simplified and shouldn't take more than a few hours. But be aware that trying to shorten the closing time before eliminating vast amounts of unnecessary work could be an exercise in futility and frustration.

### Communicating Financial Information

In many companies, limited knowledge exists not only concerning a company's financial issues, but also concerning how to interpret the information that is available. Financial people need to train others in the organization so that they understand how the specific actions they take can affect performance. Employees need to know how they are doing in terms of such things as delivery and quality, but they also ought to know whether the company is making money. What are the key elements of sales, costs and profit? What is the return on capital employed, and how is the company doing on this measure? Often, very little is understood below the level of general manager. Training should extend all the way down to the factory floor. Of course, the degrees of knowledge can be different. What's important is for people to understand the cost implications associated with things that they do and can control. In this way, Finance can have a very positive impact by providing meaningful data, as well as the training that might be needed on how to interpret it.

When it comes to financial issues, as in other areas, we've found that honesty is the best policy. If you don't share financial information, people usually will think the company is making a lot of money. If that isn't true, they need to know, so they will help do something about it. If a company is making a lot of money, management would be better off to share some of the profit, rather than try to hide the fact. After all, providing meaningful incentives can lead to even more profit.

Financial people need to understand the lean process so that they can help find ways to improve financial performance. Understanding the process will enable them to develop information and reporting systems that will be the most productive. It is as difficult to change old habits in the Finance function as it is in the other areas throughout the enterprise. If new accounting methods aren't put in place, however, the transition to lean will be extremely difficult.

## Human Resources

The Human Resources (HR) function has a major role to play, especially in supporting the cultural change aspects of the lean transformation. Our experience is that half the battle in changing to a lean environment is cultural. (The other half is the technical aspect of implementing lean programs.) Lean programs require people to think differently. Managers must give up the "command and control" approach to managing in favor of much more participative leadership styles. As teams become empowered, managers must adopt more of a "coaching" style. These changes can be very difficult for a traditional organization. The entire general management team must take the lead role in making the transformation, but HR should provide lead staff support in training, personnel changes, changing of incentive systems, and (where appropriate) discussions with labor unions.

## Training

The lean transformation requires an extensive amount of training, and training is needed in areas such as the following: Overall lean concepts, team empowerment, change management, specific lean tools (e.g. quick die change), and lean accounting. HR must work with the other members of the top management team to define the training requirements and to ensure that the programs are of high quality. At the plant level, HR needs to take the lead in ensuring that training is carried out, including the tracking of those who attend the programs. Such training includes not only the cultural change aspects of lean, but also the monitoring of specific skills training such as six sigma quality training, and the cross training of shop floor workers on each job in their department or work cell.

## Changing Incentive Systems

In many traditional companies, incentive programs reward individual workers for high productivity. One form of such a system is called a "piece-work incentive" where a worker might have a base number of parts he or she is expected to produce. When this amount is exceeded, the worker receives bonus pay. Unfortunately, individual incentive systems such as this do little to boost total output. Instead, they merely pile up work-in-progress inventory. What's worse, piece-work incentive systems often do not take quality into account, i.e. the bonus is paid even if the individual produces defective parts.

In the final analysis, individual incentive systems simply are not compatible with continuous flow production. In a continuous flow environment, an individual worker will produce only at the takt time of the entire cell or work group, rendering the individual incentive meaningless. Also, since production is done only to demand pull (via kanban) there will be times when no production takes place, and workers tackle quality projects, maintenance, or other improvement goals. Where individual incentive plans exist, it is critical to change them so that entire groups or teams rather than individuals are rewarded for high productivity.

### Policies on Workforce Changes

Lean producers normally require 25-40% fewer people to produce the same level of output as a mass producer. In an ideal world, the entire excess workforce will be absorbed through growth of the business. In cases where near-term growth is likely, we have seen companies guarantee that no worker will be laid off because of lean programs. This is the best situation and makes for an up beat policy statement.

Unfortunately, near term growth is not always on the horizon, especially in troubled or declining industries. The management team must decide how redundancies will be handled. Sometimes attrition is sufficient to handle the reductions. In other cases, companies will make a one-time cut and then declare that no other changes will be made, except by attrition. Both these approaches are strongly preferable to the "drip torture" method of continuous downsizing as lean is implemented. Individuals on the shop floor will quickly realize that lean means fewer jobs, and are likely to stop cooperating in the process. And, obviously, the drip torture method can destroy morale.

In our experience, regardless what approach is taken, it is best to be open and honest. Where redundancies are inevitable and cannot be achieved in a single cut, it is best to tell people up-front how many will be downsized and how the selection process will work (e.g. seniority, skill levels, or some other method). We have also seen that being generous with severance packages helps a lot. The additional cost to the company is modest and the good will it generates (in spite of a negative situation) is worth the extra cost.

Dealing with the concrete heads is somewhat simpler. These are people you want to leave the organization. Here again, HR should establish a severance policy and make it ready. Concrete heads are not always immediately identifiable, but usually surface in the first months after beginning the transformation. It is imperative that they leave the organization as quickly as possible since they can "poison the well." A word of caution is appropriate here. Beware of prejudging who will be a concrete head and who won't. We have been surprised in both directions—people who we thought would make the transition and don't, and vice versa. Give the transformation a few months to see who is leading the charge and who has become an anchor.

### Changing Hiring Criteria

As the transformation progresses, it will become clear that hiring criteria for new employees must change. Shop floor workers will be required to have higher skill levels, especially in reading, writing, math, and the ability to communicate their thoughts and ideas. They must also be team oriented rather than individual contributors.

The same goes for management and professional people, particularly engineers. New hires must be team oriented and must also believe in empowerment of team members at as low a level in the organization as is feasible. The "lone ranger" type generally will not fit well in the new culture.

### Union Discussions

Many companies that initiate the lean transformation are unionized. Some unions adapt quickly to the new culture and some fight it fiercely. Our recommendation with respect to discussing lean with the union leadership (and with the rank and file) is the same as above. Be open and honest about the changes, and establish (with the union) procedures for redundancy. In general, we find that workers on the shop floor, be they unionized or not, strongly prefer a lean environment because they have much more responsibility, authority, and acquire a much broader range of skills. Because workers are encouraged to think, they have more fun and experience a greater sense of fulfillment. We've often heard comments such as, "I used to hate coming to work. It was boring and unpleasant—more like a prison than a factory. Now I can't wait to get here in the morning because I have so many ideas I want to try." The resistance to lean generally comes from supervisors (foreman), middle management, and the union leadership, all of whom see in the transformation a loss of control and authority.

An open and honest discussion needs to take place that addresses the consequences the company will suffer if it does not become lean. Once a single competitor begins the journey, all will have to follow, or face a steady decline in market share. A plant with a quarter or so fewer people is better than no plant at all. Moreover, if a company starts ahead of its competition, it may be able to become lean solely through attrition. If it is late getting started, the changes may have to occur in a more draconian manner. Waiting too long could even mean closure of the factory.

## Sales and Marketing

Sales and Marketing will have the lead role in selling lean to the customer. It is critical, therefore, that Sales and Marketing be well versed in lean principles.

### Selling Lean Capabilities

Implementing the strategy of reduced manufacturing lead time requires that customers know about it and take advantage of it. Without communications programs from Sales and Marketing it will not happen. Part of the sales pitch also has to be the higher quality levels that result from going lean. You will also want to set up kanban systems with the customers so that they can pull their requirements from you. This is the best way to avoid the wild swings that can be caused by a customer's MRP system. We suggest starting with a pilot program for one or more customers so that they can become comfortable. Then watch your mass production competitors try to follow as you drop your manufacturing lead time from weeks to days and finally to less than one day. The only way they can follow is by adding huge amounts of inventory. (Unless they also become lean.)

Sales and Marketing must also sell the concept that total working capital will be reduced. Many original equipment manufacturers (OEMs) are pushing heavily for their suppliers to provide consignment inventory of 1-2 weeks and extended payment terms (e.g. 45-60 days for North America). A mistaken belief is that their costs will be lowered by this approach. The reality is that costs have merely been transferred from the OEM's P&L and balance sheet to the supplier's. No costs have been taken out of the value chain. Sooner or later these costs will reappear in the supplier's prices to the customer. The lean approach, on the other hand, actually takes cost out of the system. This benefits both customers and suppliers by lowering costs and working capital for both.

Part of the selling approach should be to convince customers to take product in smaller lots, but with more frequent delivery. For example, try going from one shipment per week to twice per week, and finally to daily deliveries. Each increment will reduce significantly the investment required in working capital for both the customer and the supplier.

Once the customer becomes comfortable with the reliability of the lean system, it will become time to sell more value-added services. For example, an OEM customer may wish to have a supplier who can provide entire subassemblies on a just-in-time basis. This is currently a major thrust of the global auto industry. A lean company is in the best position to win these contracts.

Another selling element for OEM customers is to agree on how much capacity will be allocated to the customer for a given period of time (e.g. a year). This is important to ensure that there is ample capacity available to support the customer, but not excess capacity that adds cost. We've seen OEM customer ordering patterns with violent swings, as discussed in Part II. Usually, these are caused by the customer's MRP, not by real changes in demand. In some instances an OEM customer's line rate might be 1000 units a day, but they will suddenly order at twice that rate. Upon inquiry, the cause is usually determined to be a quirk in the MRP system.

Sales and Marketing needs to take an active role in helping determine the customer's demand rate in order to be able to separate real demand from false demand.

**Sales Forecasting**

As discussed in Part II, forecasting serves a useful purpose in lean companies. It is used for capacity planning and ordering of long-lead-time materials. Even though the company will actually make product only to customer demand, the forecast can be an important tool. It is Sales and Marketing's role to provide this. Often it is based on forecasts made by customers themselves. It should be kept in mind, of course, that some can be often overly optimistic, and issue forecasts that are too high. Sales and Marketing ought to take a hard look, and add reasoned judgment to the projections. We've found that the closer the department is to the customer, the more reliable the information will be.

**Voice of the Customer for New Designs.**

Understanding customers' needs also will enable sales to give Design Engineering good direction in development of new products, and can be equally important in decisions concerning what products the lean enterprise should have in its portfolio. Sometimes a tendency exists to offer a wide range in order to be in the position to cross-sell. But an advantage may be realized with a narrow selection at lower cost. Sales and marketing should lead the way in determining the best course, and in developing exit strategies for products that are becoming obsolete. Sales and Marketing also will take the lead in performing analyses with the customer (such as Quality Function Deployment—QFD) to translate their needs into specific product attributes.

**Customer Service Organization**

Another issue regarding sales has to do with customer service (the function that interfaces with the customer on a day to day basis, taking orders and fielding inquiries). Traditionally, customer service is a sales function, but we have seen it work both as part of Sales and Marketing, or as part of the factory's Production Control function. When it is part of Production Control, the orders go straight into the production system, and all production status information is readily at hand or nearby on the shop floor. In an environment where products are manufactured and shipped in one or two days, customer inquiries on order status are usually dramatically reduced. We've seen this approach work well when the customer base is comprised primarily of OEMs. For a distribution or consumer customer base, it may be best to leave Customer Service as part of Sales and Marketing. In this case, it's often best to place the team in close proximity to Production Control—often in the same or adjacent rooms. If this is not possible because Customer Service is off site, easy-to-use communication links (including, possibly, video conferencing) are crucial to maintaining a smooth flow of information.

We wrote in Part I about Dell Computer. Dell has a system where the telephone sales people send the order directly to Production Control via Dell's internal computer system. That system also allows the customer to track his or her own order status via the Internet. So a customer can tell when the order is in production, when it has been shipped, etc. In this way, Dell has made the physical location of Customer Service irrelevant.

## Purchasing

Purchasing is one of the most critical functions in the lean transformation. In most of the factories we work with, between 35-65% of cost is in purchased materials. With so much flowing from the outside, the lean enterprise system simply will not work unless suppliers have outstanding quality and can support a just-in-time delivery system. This means that the suppliers must also become lean.

To be sure, one of Purchasing's roles in the lean organization is the same as for a traditional organization. Namely, this is to use the company's purchasing leverage to achieve a very competitive supply base. In a lean company, however, Purchasing must go further. The function must take the lead in carrying the lean message to suppliers and must also help draw in the key resources (e.g. Quality Assurance) to make the transformation occur. The task begins with the selection of suppliers that are willing and able to make the change. Our experience has been that we usually end up having fewer suppliers. When we go out into the supply base to pitch the concept, a number simply are not interested. They'd rather forgo the business than go through the effort, although we've found they won't say this directly in most cases. They simply do not or will not respond. These suppliers are not with us long. Our strategy is to work with those that will make the transition along with us. We may end up with fewer, but these become our lean enterprise partners.

## Consider Suppliers as Part of Your Value Chain

The traditional approach in Purchasing has been to consider suppliers as the enemy, and to treat them accordingly. This is not consistent with the lean approach. The lean enterprise views suppliers as critical players in the value chain from raw materials to customers. Rather than play one against another, squeezing as hard as possible to obtain the lowest price, a serious attempt is made to understand what the fair price of a component should actually be.

The Purchasing staff needs to become expert in lean production techniques so that they can give advice and counsel, and even training in some instances, in an effort to facilitate a supplier's transformation to lean. An entirely lean value chain will provide higher quality, lower cost products, along with relatively hassle free service, and just-in-time delivery. So, everyone benefits from the beginning to the end of it.

Our experience is that there are two kinds of companies. One will give a vendor a design, and ask for a bid. Others will bring their suppliers in at the beginning. They will explain their objectives and their cost targets. They will encourage the vendor to offer suggestions on changes that might be made to lower cost or make improvements that can affect performance or manufacturability. This second kind of company usually comes out ahead. It does so by optimizing the whole rather than focusing on parts. In the end, more products are sold because customers who consume the product get the best price, quality is high, and so is customer satisfaction and retention.

Lean enterprises work hard to change how they operate so

that they become more responsive to their customers. Their suppliers need to do the same. Raw materials and components at the lean enterprise are handled through kanbans. A primary goal of materials supply should be to extend this to suppliers since keeping the flow of parts running smoothly requires efficient coordination. In the ideal customer-supplier relationship, the two companies will work together to employ the same continuous flow to pull method of doing business. For example, kanbans might be sent to the supplier's warehouse where parts are pulled and sent directly to the lean enterprise's assembly floor. Kanbans might be used to notify suppliers as stocks are depleted, so that they can automatically replenish them.

### Suppliers Must Also Wage a War on Costs

Lean suppliers must also realize that in today's business environment the war on costs is constant. If a company is continually improving how it operates, which is a basic tenet of lean enterprise, its costs should come down. Raw material and purchased components also generally account for a significant percentage of cost. A reduction in these areas can be accomplished in a number of ways. It might come about, for example, by changing the way inventory is handled, as illustrated earlier. Or it could be accomplished through redesign of a product or part. Materials supply should work to integrate suppliers into the early stages of product development so that they become involved in the effort to meet price and cost goals.

### Suppliers Must Provide Just-In-Time Delivery

In the same manner that you are striving to supply your customers to JIT windows, your suppliers should deliver goods when you need them. You let them know when, where, what, and in what quantity by sending them kanbans. You may recall the example of Dell Computers. Kanbans communicate to nearby supermarkets which parts will be required to assemble a custom-tailored computer that's just been ordered. As kanbans arrive, parts are pulled and sent to the assembly shop floor.

Initially, your suppliers may supply your pull-scheduling needs out of inventory, as do many of Dell's suppliers. It is imperative, however, that the supply chain also become lean. Otherwise, cost will not be removed from the system. Eventually, you will end up paying more for components.

## Exerting Global Purchasing Leverage

Another Purchasing strategy bears mentioning. Larger companies often can save money by making global buys. Inevitably, of course, some local operations within the same organization will be able to improve on the price of certain items. Even so, we suggest resisting the temptation to break ranks and allow local Purchasing. It's usually much better to stick with the big picture. Optimizing individual parts usually does not end up optimizing the whole.

It is unfortunate but true. Unless your firm is a very large and important to the companies that supply you, you will not have the clout necessary to convince your suppliers to do business your way. For small, local companies, the ability to command and demand competitive pricing is limited. In many cases, though, Purchasing cooperatives can be put together so that needs are lumped together to get better pricing. This can be win-win for companies that form co-ops, and the suppliers that sell to them.

## Dealing with Long Lead Time Items

What about long lead time items? Some suppliers may require an order to be placed well ahead, often 16-20 weeks or more. But often the final number will not have to be firmed up until, perhaps, four weeks ahead of time. The advance order in effect reserves some of that supplier's capacity. By staying on top of orders such as this and re-forecasting, Purchasing may be able to eliminate some risk by fine tuning the order.

What if you order components that you believe will be needed in six months, but when the time comes, your customers don't order from you? This easily can happen with electronic components such as certain microprocessors, displays, and memory chips. The fact is, it may be impossible to avoid being left with outdated parts. We suggest you weigh the trade off between the cost of components ordered direct, well in advance, and the higher cost but shorter delivery times when they're purchased through distributors. When you make your calculations, don't forget that the possibility of being left with outdated inventory is only one downside of buying ahead. The room required to store inventory, as well as personnel and systems to manage it, also should be considered.

In closing this section, let us say that we believe that someday the companies that supply your firm will transform their own enterprise to lean. When they do, you'll already be ready to reap the benefits.

## Lean Organization

There's an additional critical aspect of a lean enterprise that ought to be mentioned here. Namely, this is a flat organization structure without layer upon layer of management. Figure 3.1 opposite this page illustrates one example of a "before lean" and "after lean" management structure in one operation—a subsidiary with $120 million in sales. The company had four layers of management between the general manager and shop floor employees at the time lean transformation was begun. Today, it has only two. Costs have been reduced, but more important,

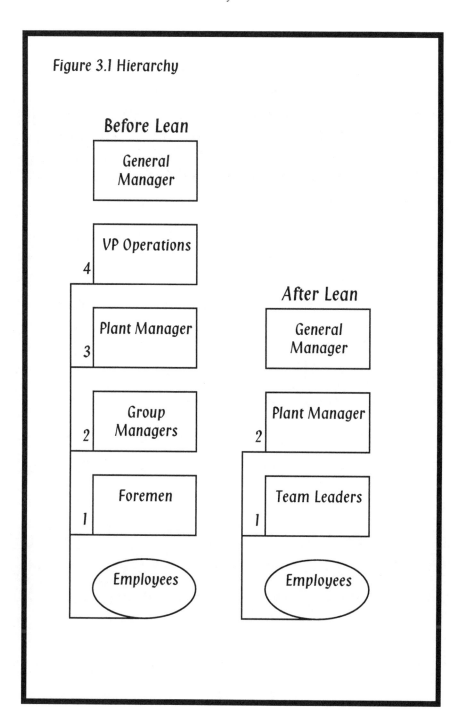

Figure 3.1 Hierarchy

**Before Lean**

General Manager

4 | VP Operations

3 | Plant Manager

2 | Group Managers

1 | Foremen

Employees

**After Lean**

General Manager

2 | Plant Manager

1 | Team Leaders

Employees

decision-making time has been speeded up tremendously, and bureaucracy and paperwork cut significantly.

Was this action difficult? Only because there was a management mindset that said the management layers were necessary, and also because the people in those layers fought a pitched battle to demonstrate that their roles were absolutely necessary. Nevertheless, a new general manager was brought in whose first action was to remove the unnecessary layers. The organization never skipped a beat, and it never looked back.

# PART IV

## Sustaining the Change

If you've taken in most of what has been written to this point, you now know a great deal about lean production and what comprises a lean enterprise. You'll probably agree that the concept is amazingly simple. All areas of the company work together with the same goal as a shared vision. Because the vision either manifests or falls short in assembly and production, most of the remainder of the company is organized to facilitate continuous flow, defect-free assembly and production that is timed and tuned to match output with customer demand.

Why is this so difficult to accomplish and sustain?

Egos, personal agendas, lack of understanding, and an almost fanatical clinging to traditional ways of doing things, and the past in general.

After dozens of lean enterprise initiatives in plants and businesses around the world, we have found that initial gains come relatively easily. The difficulty lies in maintaining those gains, and sustaining the transformation through the inevitable backlash by middle management, as well as the lethargy and complacency that can easily descend upon an organization.

### Five Key Factors for Lean Enterprise Success

It is our experience that five factors are required for a successful, ongoing transformation:

*(1) Management must have a strategic vision of what the organization is moving toward and will become.* The top management team must be able to see how the company will be different, and what, for example, the primary advantages over competition will be. This strategic vision must be held firmly in mind, and communicated to management and staff throughout the

organization so that it becomes a shared vision all are working toward.

*(2) There must be strong line management leadership committed to change.* This is essential. Leaders of the transformation must be chosen carefully. They must have the imagination necessary to grasp "what can be," and share top managements' vision of the company's future. An important aspect of the makeup of leaders selected to institute change should be that they focus on the future and the possibilities it holds, rather than on the past and its time-honored traditions.

*(3) Expert training and support likely will be needed in order to get started.* This may require bringing in a seasoned lean transformation expert to help in at least the initial, start up and training phase. After training has taken place, those left in charge should have enough knowledge to be self-correcting in the event that the transformation strays off course. It also may help to have a sounding board, someone who has been through transformation, who can be called upon periodically for advice and counsel.

*(4) Aggressive lean enterprise performance targets and tracking.* People need to know what is expected of them, and they need goals and objectives to shoot for. This might take the form of specific objectives to do with reductions in throughput time, inventory turns, scrap reduction, and returns due to defects. Goals in general can be important motivators and will form a major topic of discussion in this section.

*(5) Impatience.* Impatience by management to see the organization move ahead and deliver tangible results. Impatience means that foot-dragging will not be tolerated. It means that concrete heads will not be given much time to get on board. In its most productive form, impatience should translate into a fire that is lit under the organization to realize the vision.

Indeed, we have discovered what we now refer to as "The

Lean Enterprise Paradox." This is that line management must be simultaneously directive and empowering. It would seem that these traits do not go hand in hand. But our experience is that strong leadership is required; leadership that is unambiguous, leadership that is clear about the lean enterprise path. At the same time, a leader continually must empower teams along the way. Teams must be handed complete authority to carry out tasks they have been assigned. They must be empowered.

We have found that when the five lean enterprise factors have been present, impressive results have been achieved, and the lean transformation has been sustained. When one or more factors have been missing, lean transformation has fallen short of our expectations and desires.

A word of caution may be appropriate. Your impatience, while needed and potentially constructive, should be tempered with a healthy dose of realism. An important decision you'll need to make is how quickly to move ahead once lean transformation has begun. In your manufacturing and assembly operations, this will depend largely on the ability of the supporting infrastructure to keep up. If you have one or two lines, infrastructure may not be an issue. But the situation can be considerably different if you have 6, 10, 20, or more assembly lines in a given complex. Maintenance and material handling are likely to become stressed as the conversion of one line after another takes place.

### Factor Number One: A Strategic Vision

Knowing what you now know about lean enterprise, what would you want your company to look like if you were starting it today from scratch? If you were running a computer company, for example, would your vision be of Dell, with its continuous flow to customer demand method of supply, manufacturing, and distribution, or would it be modeled after one of the more traditionally run computer sales and assembly businesses?

If you answered Dell, how does this translate into your industry? How would you set it up?

This should be your vision.

To realize it will require dramatic change, and change can be difficult at best. To some it can be frightening. For many, comfort can be found in the known and the expected, even when the known and expected are not all that wonderful. Perhaps this is why incumbent politicians often have a big advantage over challengers. It is certainly a reason the transformation into a lean enterprise is extremely difficult. Given this reality, how do you get people to accept your new vision? What can you do to get their attention and blast them out of their complacency?

One catalyst can be a real or perceived crisis. This might be that your company no longer is able to compete effectively. Let's look directly into the eyeballs of reality. Over time, organizations can become overstaffed. Positions that once served a useful purpose may become outmoded by changes in technology or the marketplace. Yet the people who fill them remain on the payroll. Unless you actually do happen to be starting an organization from scratch, nowadays it is probably quite likely that your organization has too much fat, too much waste, too many workers, too much duplication and too much equipment devoted to activities that do not create value. This is doubly true if a competitor happens to adopt a course of lean transformation. Unless you do, too, your company may not survive. If the situation in your company has not yet reached a state of crisis, we suggest you consider trumping it up to make it seem so. If you wait, you may well face a real crisis later that will be nearly impossible to overcome.

Last year, AT&T announced a major downsizing of 18,000 employees.[27] AT&T Chairman C. Michael Armstrong was quoted as saying that he'd not only reduce his work force by as much as 14% but would also offer a panoply of new services, including cheap phone calls over the Internet and wireless phones that will receive calls free. The article also said that the company would spend billions to upgrade its national communications network, which had been surpassed in efficiency by newer systems.

Today, such a scenario is hardly new. If it were not for the magnitude of this overhaul, it's doubtful this story would have created headlines at all, at least not in newspapers beyond the company's headquarters city. In this new age of global competition, only those companies offering the highest quality at the lowest prices will survive. This is what AT&T failed to do in the years proceeding this writing, and the company's share of the long distance market has dropped accordingly.

If your company happens to be in the same boat as AT&T, in what appears to be a do-or-die position, rather than rail against this, you might actually consider yourself fortunate. You have in place a catalyst for change, a fire that's been lit under every manager and worker who wants to remain gainfully employed. If the business is in trouble, and if this puts their livelihood in jeopardy, all have an incentive to work together in a spirit of absolute cooperation to correct the situation. Lean enterprise is a survival strategy they may thankfully embrace. At the very least, it is a potential lifesaver they can hardly afford to reject. Once they see it this way, chances are most of them will pull together to do what it takes to make the transformation. The odds are excellent that the company will emerge from this trying time stronger and more competitive than ever.

What if your business does not face an immediate crisis? What if the transformation you wish to undertake is primarily a defensive measure you'd like to take in order to remain competitive, or an offensive measure that will strengthen the company's position? Opposition likely will be strong.

It is not likely to be the workers who resist transformation. We've seen the attitudes of workers change from somber or glum, to enthusiastic and upbeat, in a matter of days—weeks at most. Our post transformation surveys indicate they often believe that they aren't working as hard as they once did. Employee job satisfaction figures usually soar. Workers feel, indeed are, empowered. This feeling, and the attitude that goes with it, should be a key component of your all-important vision for the future.

## Factor Number Two: Strong Line Management

Line management is the link to strategy, and strong line management leadership is absolutely critical to a successful lean enterprise program. Without its full commitment, failure is almost certain. As has been discussed, becoming a lean enterprise involves major cultural change, and this requires perseverance. Moreover, cultural and technical roadblocks are not all that must be cleared away. Floor layouts, people, multiple levels of bureaucracy, systems such as accounting and MRP, all will have to be changed. The truth is, lean enterprise "goes against the grain" of just about everything that companies have held dear about traditional mass manufacturing since the days of Henry Ford's first assembly lines.

This is one of the most critical lessons we've learned: *The inertia factor of a traditional manufacturer cannot be underestimated.* With people who do not want to change, it is a classic case of the old saying, "You can lead a horse to water, but you can't make him drink." The truth is, more than inertia is at work. The traditional organization will fight back.

Let's say a very successful kaizen event is held with huge improvements in performance. Enthusiasm will be high among the participants. They will be charged up and ready to find more

Figure 4.1, Lean Transformation Backlash

85+ Years of Mass Manufacturing Inertia

Organization Backlash

85+ Years of Mass Manufacturing Inertia

Lean Enterprise goes against the grain of traditional mass manufacturing

ways to improve, more muda to be cut. This is probably the moment a backlash from the traditional organization will occur.

Why? Turf has been threatened. For better or worse, managers perceive that they have lost control. A "tug of war" between early adapters and concrete heads will ensue. About 80% of the organization will be caught smack in the middle. The outcome will either be success or failure, and this will depend on the actions taken by line management.

Figure 4.2 shows actual data collected in separate instances. Using inventory turns as a key measure, the motivated team went from about nine turns to 23 turns at the plant level in less than two years. The resistant team made no progress at all despite an an enormous and expensive amount of consulting input. This

**Figure 4.2, Enthusiastic vs. Resistant Management**

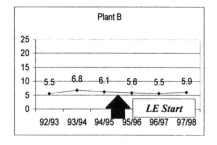

leads to what we call the "Lean Enterprise Paradox." Line management "style" must be simultaneously directive and empowering.

The words "directive" and "empowering" simply do not sound as if they ought to go together. But in this case they do.

Strong leadership is required, leadership that is crystal clear about the lean enterprise path. At the same time, the leader must continually empower the teams along the way. Being simply "directive" in management style is not enough.

We have literally seen two extremes: A motivated management team, combined with a little bit of expert input, will produce phenomenal results in a short period of time. In other words, motivated line management has a tremendous amplifying effect on expert consulting input. (See Figure 4.3 below.) By contrast, a line management team that does not want to change will nullify the effects of a huge amount of expert input.

**Figure 4.3, Management Team Impact**

Our advice is not to waste time with people who will not change. Moreover, be aware that you have a big problem on your hands if many of your plant managers falls into this category, and and even bigger one if you have a concrete head in a general manager position. All probably will have to be replaced, or transformation at the plant level will be stifled. (See Figure 4.4)

Even if everyone else wants to change, the effort will fail.

We say this from painful experience. In all cases, satisfactory progress was not made until the management situation was dealt with and the right individuals put into place.

**Figure 4.4, Don't Waste Time on Concrete Heads**

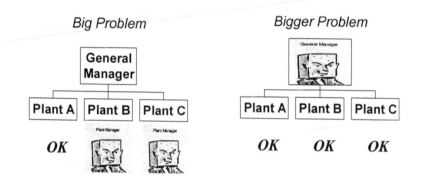

It's important that once you have the right people in place, they have tools they can use besides a whip. Psychological motivators, for example, can be powerful. The need to keep the corporate ship afloat can go a long way toward squashing the mutineers. A shared objective can be a powerful rallying point. It can help foster the creation of esprit d'corps and the feeling on the part of individuals of being a part of something bigger than themselves. We often refer to this as the *big goal*. For a football team it might be the Super Bowl. In tennis, the Davis Cup. In soccer, the World Cup.

Change can happen quickly and be truly dramatic when an organization embraces a *big goal* that must be achieved within a relatively short period of time. In its most effective form, what we're writing about might be compared to the challenge presented by President Kennedy, that the United States should work to land a man on the moon within the decade of the sixties. This came along at a time when the nation was worried that it may have fallen behind in terms of technology and the race into space. The Soviet Union had launched a satellite called Sputnik. People could go into their backyards at night and see it, circling the globe. The United States had no satellites. Along with the Cold War and nuclear missiles, Sputnik provided a source of palpable anxiety. The time was ripe to announce such a goal, and it worked. The nation indeed pulled together and the space race was won. This is what you want your company to do: Pull together and win.

What might your *big goal* be? It could be to become the preferred supplier of whatever you make in your particular industry. It might be to overtake the number two spot, or it might be number ten that you're shooting for. It could be to eliminate back orders, or to have the best on-time record, or to win a particular award, or to reduce customer complaints a hundred fold. Whatever is relevant and meaningful to your company and the business will do, as long as it makes sense to use lean transformation as a strategy to reach it.

A few more thoughts on identifying a *big goal* may be helpful. What you decided upon may be something that hinges on an advantage over the competition that you now are not in position to offer. Going lean should open up the possibilities. The key will be to determine which is most significant in the minds of your managers, and your customers. Take some time and figure out what these potential advantages are. One may be that you'll be able to offer quicker delivery. Or a lower defect rate. Or the ability for customers to select the specific product options that they want. Maybe you'll use increased productivity to undercut the competition in terms of price. Decide all the practical advantages that your firm will be in position to offer, and put something in writing that outlines this. Keep an open mind about what may actually be the single most compelling competitive advantage.

Circulate the document to the managers of your firm, or call them together and give them a presentation. Tell them you haven't decided what core value the company should hang its hat on once the transformation to lean is made, and you want their help.

This will do a couple of things. It will call attention to the strategic advantages your company will enjoy, and it will bring managers together in an effort to decide how best to capitalize on them. If all goes well, the effort to put a finger on the most important value may provide the mechanism needed to rally them together in a way that will result in an easier transformation. People feel good when their help and opinions are sought. Besides, you do want their ideas, the more the better, and their participation should cause them to feel a closer bond to the company. After all, this is to be their core value. It is to be what they offer customers above all else. You want them to feel ownership. If they do, they're likely to put their full efforts behind whatever needs to be accomplished, lean transformation in this case, in order to deliver.

### Factor Number Three: Expert Training and Support

Expert training and support will be required in order for you to get going, especially if little lean enterprise experience exists in your company. You may have to bring in someone from the outside to help with this.

The training step should not, however, be belabored. You will need enough to get started, and enough knowledge on site on an ongoing basis to be self-correcting when a false step or a mistake is made. If your value stream has been mapped correctly, you'll know where you're headed. If you get off track, you simply need to back up to the logical place from which to start moving forward again. Under the heading of support, though, there should be someone for local plant personnel to call upon if they do become stumped and find themselves painted into a corner with no apparent way to arrive back on track.

Where does the required lean expertise come from? Typically, it comes from people already on staff, as well as new hires, who have prior experience with lean. It can also come from outside consultants, from the Toyota Supplier Support Center, and from the Lean Enterprise Institute. (In the transformations we've undertaken, it has come mostly from the first two.)

It makes sense to begin the transformation in the area closest to the customer. In manufacturing, this is final assembly. It follows that it also makes sense to begin the training program with the personnel who work in this area. Our goal has been to develop a "picture" of a lean producer in their minds. Essentially, we attempt to communicate what we shared with you in Part I, focusing on the basic philosophies of the lean enterprise and the six fundamental characteristics of a lean producer.

## Factor Number Four: Aggressive Performance Targets

The following measurements have been useful in tracking lean enterprise implementation. They have been designed to take advantage of existing plant-level data and to minimize the amount of additional information to be collected.

### (1) Inventory turns (Figure 4.5)

Inventory is tracked using an inventory turns chart. Information is presented as a 12-month rolling trend line. Each month we add a month and delete a month.

The inventory turns calculation is made based on the past 12 months' sales, and the inventory balance at the end of the current month. For example, August 1999 turns would be calculated based on sales from August 1998 through August 1999, divided by the August 1999 inventory balance. The goal is to achieve an improvement of at least 20 to 30% inventory turns, year-on-year.

**Figure 4.5**

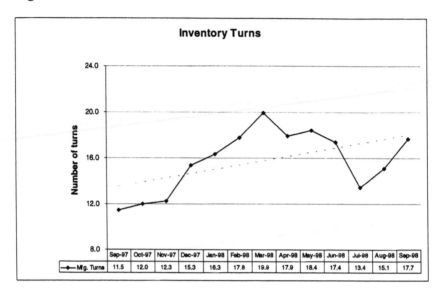

**Figure 4.6**

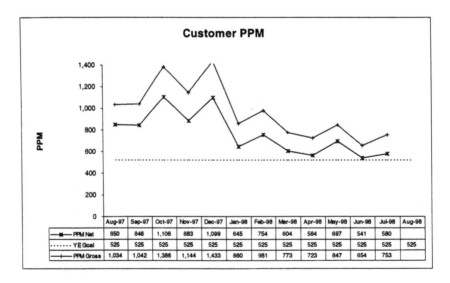

**(2) *Customer PPM (Figure 4.6)***

Customers' product returns are measured in PPMs. Two measures are charted monthly, total returns from customers versus total amount shipped to such customers in the month that a shipment took place. Thus, we have to refer to shipping dates. We also show gross returns and net returns (subtracting out the "no defect found" items).

Information is presented for the last 12 months with the objective of viewing a trend line. Each month we add a month, and delete a month. The objective is to achieve a 50% reduction year-on-year. The chart should contain a goal line showing the 50% year-over-year improvement target. (See Figure 4.6)

**(3) *On-time-delivery (OTD) to customer want date***

The objective is to measure the trend with an ultimate objective of reaching 100% on-time delivery to customers' want dates.

Monthly information is presented in a rolling 12 month chart. A month is added and deleted each month. The graph may have a horizontal line representing the goal for the year (i.e. 95%).

**Figure 4.7**

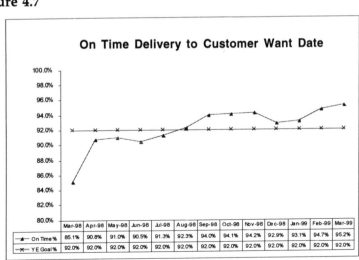

| | Mar-98 | Apr-98 | May-98 | Jun-98 | Jul-98 | Aug-98 | Sep-98 | Oct-98 | Nov-98 | Dec-98 | Jan-99 | Feb-99 | Mar-99 |
|---|---|---|---|---|---|---|---|---|---|---|---|---|---|
| On Time % | 85.1% | 90.8% | 91.0% | 90.5% | 91.3% | 92.3% | 94.0% | 94.1% | 94.2% | 92.9% | 93.1% | 94.7% | 95.2% |
| YE Goal % | 92.0% | 92.0% | 92.0% | 92.0% | 92.0% | 92.0% | 92.0% | 92.0% | 92.0% | 92.0% | 92.0% | 92.0% | 92.0% |

## (4) LE financial performance measures: (Figure 4.7)

• *Direct materials as percentage of sales*: This measurement is calculated by dividing the monthly material component of standard cost, plus its variances, by monthly net sales. The graph includes the last 12 months performance. The objective of having this measurement is not only to observe the absolute value but also its trend in the 12-month period. An objective for reduction needs to be established.

• *Direct labor and variable overhead as percentage of sales:* These measurements are calculated using actual monthly direct labor and variable overhead, including variances divided monthly by net production sales. The two measurements are presented in the same graph. A need exists to have a definition of what is included in the variable overhead so that there is clear understanding when analysis of the chart is performed. The graph includes the past twelve month performance. The objective is not only to observe the absolute value, but also the 12-month trend. An objective for reduction also should be established.

• *Fixed overhead and SG&A as percentage of sales:* These measurements will be calculated by using actual monthly fixed manufacturing overhead and SG&A divided by monthly sales. The two measurements are presented in the same graph. A need exists to have a clear definition of what is included in fixed overhead when performing chart analysis. The same is true for SG&A. The graph includes the past twelve month performance figures. The objective is not only to observe the absolute value, but also its trend in the 12-month period. An objective for reduction needs to be established.

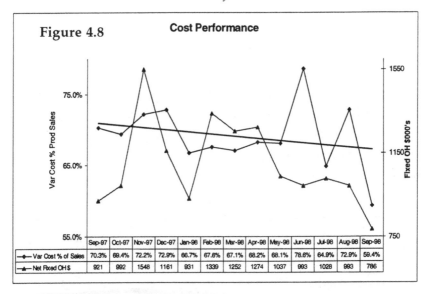

Figure 4.8 — Cost Performance

| | Sep-97 | Oct-97 | Nov-97 | Dec-97 | Jan-98 | Feb-98 | Mar-98 | Apr-98 | May-98 | Jun-98 | Jul-98 | Aug-98 | Sep-98 |
|---|---|---|---|---|---|---|---|---|---|---|---|---|---|
| Var Cost % of Sales | 70.3% | 69.4% | 72.2% | 72.9% | 66.7% | 67.6% | 67.1% | 68.2% | 68.1% | 78.6% | 64.9% | 72.9% | 59.4% |
| Net Fixed OH$ | 921 | 992 | 1548 | 1161 | 931 | 1339 | 1252 | 1274 | 1037 | 993 | 1028 | 993 | 786 |

• *OPBIT and PBT Return on sales:* These measurements are calculated by using actual monthly OPBIT and PBT divided by monthly sales. The two measurements are presented in the same graph. The graph will include the last twelve months performance for the plant.

• *Working capital and fixed capital turns:* These measurements are calculated by using actual monthly sales divided by monthly working capital and fixed capital. The reason monthly values are used has to do with seasonality in many products/plants. This can cause wide variation in working capital needs. If we used 12 month averages, a variation might be masked. In this case, the effect on return on capital employed (ROCE) would be more difficult to analyze. Working capital turns allow for analysis of capital needs as sales vary throughout the year. The graph presents the last 12 months performance for the business.

• *Total capital employed turns:* This measurement is calculated by using actual monthly sales divided by total capital employed. The graph presents the last thirteen months performance for the business.

• *Operating annualized ROCE:* This measurement is calculated using the actual last twelve months operating profit divided by current month average assets employed. The rolling twelve months is calculated by adding the latest monthly OPBIT to the last 12 months and deleting the same month value for the prior year. The number thus calculated is useful as an indicator of the return on actual financing funds for the business. The graph includes the last 12 months performance for the business.

• *Operating monthly ROCE:* This measurement is calculated using current month operating profit divided by current month average assets employed (divided by 12). The number is an indicator of the monthly return on actual financing funds for the business. The graph includes the last 13 months performance for the business. The objective of having these measurements is to allow for comparing the monthly ROCE value for the current month with the equivalent value a year earlier.

**Figure 4.9**

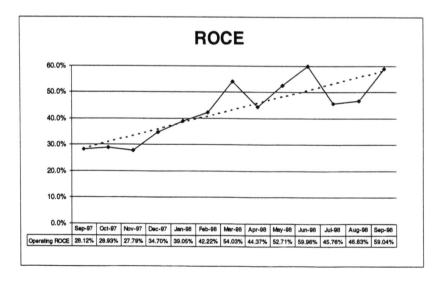

| Operating ROCE | Sep-97 | Oct-97 | Nov-97 | Dec-97 | Jan-98 | Feb-98 | Mar-98 | Apr-98 | May-98 | Jun-98 | Jul-98 | Aug-98 | Sep-98 |
|---|---|---|---|---|---|---|---|---|---|---|---|---|---|
| | 28.12% | 28.93% | 27.79% | 34.70% | 39.05% | 42.22% | 54.03% | 44.37% | 52.71% | 59.96% | 45.76% | 46.83% | 59.04% |

Collectively, these measurements allow a complete performance evaluation. You will want to continue measuring as the transformation proceeds to gauge progress, and after the transformation is complete to assure that gains are maintained.

## Factor Number Five: Impatience

Impatience should lead to action when you start to hear, "You don't understand. We are different." Or, "If we do that, it will disrupt the hierarchy of the organization." Impatience means that concrete heads will not be given much time to get on board. Anyone who identifies with the concrete heads described in Part I should start pulling together a resume.

High-level leaders might take part in individual Kaizen events. Top managers need to frequently visit plants that are in the process of transformation, and discuss progress or the lack thereof with the manager in charge. Praise or impatience should be expressed.

On the local level, plant managers need to take at least a daily walk through the organization. They need to hand out positive strokes where progress is apparent, and express displeasure with a lack of results.

Senior management should demonstrate impatience by regularly reviewing progress reports and making it known they've been reviewed. A positive trend, or the lack of one, should be noted. If tangible results aren't seen at the plant level within three to six months, something is wrong. More than likely, the wrong team, or individual, has been selected to lead the charge. It's time to reevaluate.

Remember to keep this in mind. If you move too slowly in transforming to lean, valuable momentum and enthusiasm can be lost. If you move too quickly, inevitable glitches, and the inability of materials supply and maintenance to keep up, can give naysayers gasoline to pour on the fire of discontent. Count on it. There will be naysayers. Be impatient, and also make sure the infrastructure can support the transformation.

## Communications

A final tip: Communications can play an important role in helping the organization jell and rally to accomplish the lean transformation. So use every tool you can, from newsletters, to strategy documents, to brochures, videos and advertising, in order to spread the word, and turn up the heat. Nothing makes something so real as putting it in writing. An ad in your industry's trade journal signals that you're deadly serious, not only to customers, but to employees. So what if your competitors find out what you're up to—in the spirit of Toyota, why worry? By the time they're able to copy you, if they even try, you'll be light years ahead of them.

Δ Δ Δ

## Parting Thoughts and Comments

As this book draws to a close, let's take a few pages to summarize the key points we've tried to convey, and to give you a glimpse of what the ultimate lean organization of the future might be. First and foremost, perhaps, is to understand that lean enterprise is much more than simply a formula for operational excellence. It is the ultimate strategic weapon.

### The Value of Lean Enterprise

When everything is said and done, what consumers want when they buy a product is one that performs the tasks they need done, works when it is supposed to, and costs as little as possible. They want it now, and do not wish to wait. Of course, they want service when needed, and they want their questions answered promptly and correctly. But they don't really care about guarantees or warranties, per se. What they want are no problems. Having to return something to be fixed, even at no charge, is a problem. They prefer zero defects from the outset.

Lean enterprise can fulfill these customer desires. Through lean transformation, the time required from order-to-delivery can be cut from weeks or months to hours. Because quality will be built in rather than inspected in, returns due to defects will be virtually eliminated. If you wish, prices can be slashed because the resources needed for manufacturing will be cut significantly. Money once tied up in inventory will be set free; space requirements cut in half. Customers can be given the option of configuring their own product because the one they buy will not be built until they order it, so only the product features they are willing to pay for can be bolted on or loaded in, as the unit glides along the river of continuous flow. Like a Taco Bell restaurant, a customer's order appears where workers who will assemble the product can see it. The framework or housing of the product is placed on the line, and the order, called a kanban, travels with the housing to tell each operator the model and variation to build. Your workers won't miss a beat. They pull and place the right parts picked from strategically located bins. When the assembled product arrives at the end of the line, it is wrapped, packaged, and shipped—perhaps by overnight delivery service. As your assembly operation uses up components, kanbans will be sent to your suppliers letting them know to restock.

In summary, how lean enterprise works is simple: Define value from the customer's point of view. Design in and build in quality. Eliminate anything and everything that doesn't create or add value. Make the creation of value flow evenly and continuously, starting with raw materials and suppliers as sources, or tributaries, and moving down-stream so that everything comes together into a river of production and distribution that empties into customers' hands precisely at the speed of consumption.

We're convinced this is the future of business and industry. You can be the first in your field, or you can wait, in which case you may find yourself trying to use old, conventional methods to stay afloat. This will mean building up inventory so that you can ship what customers want when they want it. It may mean cutting your margins to the bone to match the prices offered by a competitor operating with less labor and overhead. In a stressed environment, one that is undergoing rapid change as appears to be the case now in the world of business and industry, seemingly small differences can translate into big advantages. What makes lean enterprise a big gun is that it offers much more than small differences. It can bring about large ones that may well enable you to take the lead.

### Keep a Vision Firmly in Mind

The lean enterprise will be exceptionally neat and clean, even if it is employed in what is normally considered a messy business. Products are built just in time (JIT), and only to customer demand. Six sigma quality is designed into the products and built into manufacturing processes. Empowered teams on the shop floor in the case of a manufacturing operation, or wherever value for customers is being created in a service business, make key decisions. When a problem is spotted, the team decides how to fix it. There is no need for management to be called in except in rare instances when problems cannot be solved within the team. In an assembly operation, for example, workers are obligated to stop the line if they see a quality defect situation. The line remains shut down until the problem is fixed.

One result of empowered teams is that the lean enterprise is less hierarchical than traditional businesses. No need exists for layers leading up a pyramid to the person at the top. Such a bureaucracy would render rapid, on-the-spot decision making impossible. It is also expensive.

Visual management is used to track performance and to give workers feedback at regular intervals concerning performance.

The final fundamental of the lean enterprise is the relentless pursuit of perfection. This characteristic undergirds all others. Players are never satisfied with the progress they've made; never willing to rest on laurels. The culture ensures a continual and constant search for better ways to cut waste, improve quality, cut inventory, and to do things better, quicker, faster, easier. This pursuit becomes institutionalized in systems and procedures.

## Strong Leadership is Essential

It has been our experience that companies find it difficult to separate the tasks of leading the effort, and making it happen. The leader of the organization will establish the vision and be the motivating force behind the implementation process. But leaders will not make the transition happen all by themselves. In addition to a leader in each location, a team dedicated to this task will be required if a commitment has been made to "make the change" within a short period of time. This team must have the full support of local and top management. It is essential that the rest of the organization understand this, and that the team be given the green light to do whatever is required to carry out its mission.

When compared to a traditional business, a lean enterprise is one that has been turned upside down. Departments and managers exist to support the shop floor, not the other way around—because manufacturing and assembly is where the money is made. Among executives who have undergone transformation, almost without exception, concrete heads are viewed as the most serious obstacles. Yet, it is possible to turn some around. It may be helpful to recall the stages they will pass through. Denial is followed by anger, bargaining, depression, and finally, acceptance. If you can bring a concrete head this far, you've won a new lean player. But you'll probably have to stay at it. A few confrontations and a few heart-to-heart talks likely will be required. Decide how much time and how much rope you're going to give. Some people cannot, or will not, change.

Let people know what to expect. Let them know that you expect some will be early adapters, and embrace the change. You'll be delighted for them to be out there leading the charge. But you also know others will have difficulty. Remind them that a gap exists between stimulus and response. How they use this is key because in that fraction of a second, they have the power to choose. Urge them to take a breath, think, and follow a considered approach.

### The Lean Transformation Process in a Nutshell

Get everyone together and let them know what is going to

happen and what to expect. Plans, objectives, strategies, and the reasons for the transformation should be communicated. Create a vision for the immediate future, a road map that will eliminate as much uncertainty as possible. People need to understand why the decision to go lean is essential to remaining competitive. They need to know that it is the only sure way to achieve the company's goals. It also will be helpful for them to know that the transformation will affect them in many good ways. Their value as workers will be enhanced because they will receive cross training that will make them multi skilled. They can expect satisfaction with their jobs to increase. A cleaner, safer working environment will be created. The company should grow and expand, creating opportunities, some of which may flow to them.

In a manufacturing facility, the place to begin the transformation is in final assembly. You'll want to be able to measure progress, so decide what measurements to take, such as throughput time and direct and indirect labor requirements. The segmentation between direct and indirect labor will become diminished in importance as your organization becomes lean. The important thing to consider is the overall number of people required to get a product out the door and into the hands of the customer. In many cases today, direct labor constitutes less than 10% of the cost of product. Productivity measurement strictly in terms of direct labor does not give a complete picture, and may mask actions that need to be taken because it focuses attention on a limited aspect of an operation.

## Expanding Lean Throughout the Company

Expansion of lean into other areas of the organization calls for flattening out the hierarchy, shifting decision making to those closest to a situation, and operating through empowered teams. Process or industrial engineers should almost literally live in the factory and come to view inventory as something to be purged because inventory hides problems. They need to pay attention to material handling. Bins of components have to be replenished while operators are working so that flow isn't interrupted. Lines that come from different directions to merge may require special attention. Visual aids that show operators the assembly procedure, for example, may have to be laid out in mirror images.

The way quality assurance people work will shift. Verifying that a product was built correctly by inspecting it is a non value-added activity, so the move must be from an inspection culture to one that insures that the process is stable and consistently effective.

There is a need for a daily meeting between operators and line leaders. The group needs to look at its performance from the day before, and at production goals for the day ahead. Work assignments are reviewed and special instructions noted.

Once a week, groups also meet to discuss performance. This forum is used for suggestions on how to improve output and quality levels.

Human resources will become deeply involved with training. Every shop floor worker should be trained in every operation so that they will be able to rotate and to flex when called upon. Training on interpersonal skills will likely be needed.

It will be up to sales and marketing to sell lean capabilities and benefits to the customer—higher quality, shorter lead times, less inventory. Customers taking product in large quantities might be approached about leveling out orders so that product is taken in smaller quantities more frequently.

Purchasing must also learn to think differently. The lean enterprise takes the long view, and considers suppliers to be partners. To this end, suppliers should be integrated into the early stages of product development so that they become involved in the effort to meet price and cost goals. As Sales and Marketing must carry the message to customers, Purchasing must carry it to suppliers.

Empowered teams are fundamental in the design of new products. Teams should be comprised of representatives of all areas of the business that have a stake in a product, including the customer, because the end product will benefit from the different perspectives. Products should be designed for ease of manufacturing, for example, and this requires a clear understanding of the manufacturing process.

The financial systems of a traditional business are not well oriented to the lean enterprise, which likely will mean an overhaul will be required in this area. When a factory employs continuous flow, the time an individual spends to produce a certain number of units is no longer an issue. Standard cost systems are eliminated in favor of simple throughput cost accounting.

The situation is similar with inventory. If there are no batches of inventory waiting to move from one operation to the next, it makes no sense to gather the information. Work in process (WIP) won't disappear completely, but the amount will be small and shouldn't vary much from one day, week, or month to the next.

Incentive programs that reward individual workers for high output productivity will need to be revamped. It will make sense to change incentive plans so that groups or teams are rewarded for high productivity, rather than individuals.

## Putting to Work the Power of Purpose

Empowered workers and teams perform especially well when they share a sense of commitment and dedication. A big difference will be apparent, and productivity will soar, if they have pride in their work, feel that what they do is important, and believe that the company they work for makes a significant contribution to society or to the quality of life.

This same sense of dedication can also come about when an organization is fighting for survival. It is often true that people pull together in extraordinary circumstances. It will help if a reason can be identified that generates a sense of urgency. Communications play an important role in getting the word out, and in so doing helps the organization pull together to accomplish the objective. By going public and telling the world what you are up to, your own employees and executives will be put on notice that you are absolutely serious. Anyone stuck in denial will have a hard time staying there.

In our experience, top management must have a clear strategic vision of the future based on the competitive advantages that lean enterprise will bring. Line management throughout the organization must provide strong leadership and be committed to change. Leaders of the transformation must share the vision, and be able to see the possibilities that the future holds. They must be oriented toward "what can be," rather than "what has always been."

## The Ultimate Lean Organization

Traditionally, organizations are built around well-defined functions such as manufacturing, finance, human resources, engineering, and purchasing. Their structure is hierarchical. The ultimate lean organization, on the other hand, will not have traditional levels. It will have two distinct areas, one devoted to business leadership and strategy, and the other to operations. Hierarchical positions or functions will not exist as traditionally defined. Rather, different individuals will provide the particular skills required by the business.

Different aspects of this ultimate lean organization have been tried and tested in the many transformations in which we've participated, and one is currently moving forward with the overall structure described here. It has about 1,000 employees at a single site, and yet has demonstrated that the number of personnel required to operate effectively is substantially less than needed in a traditional organization. The work gets done, and people do not feel pushed. On the contrary, the ability to respond has increased. Workers have more flexibility to serve customer needs. People almost always work together in a spirit of harmony. They feel involved and committed to their company and customers. Job satisfaction is high. In some areas, reductions of personnel have reached 40% below what otherwise would be needed. Bureaucracy has been eliminated, and this has been accompanied by a dramatically increased ability to respond to customer requests and problems.

Briefly, here are the characteristics of the ultimate lean organization:

(1) No "walls" will exist between disciplines (operations, quality assurance, human resources, finance, etc.). All are part of one team.

(2) Only two "layers" exist—business leadership, and operations.

(3) Each operation is as integrated as is feasible and has all the disciplines required to produce products. This includes line personnel, maintenance, material handlers, quality assurance personnel, and team leaders, as well as support disciplines such as industrial and product engineering, customer service, scheduling, and sourcing.

(4) Activities are tracked by visual methods so that all process personnel can see where things stand at any given moment.

(5) The leader of an operation has full responsibility for it, and represents his or her organization in the company's leadership.

(6) The leadership team includes the facility's general manager,

the leaders of each operation, and the leaders of quality assurance, finance and human resources. If the research and development, engineering, purchasing and sales disciplines are present at a facility, these are also incorporated into the leadership team.

The ultimate lean organization will be clearly focused on customers. Line operators will visit customers regularly to investigate and gather information about quality issues when they arise, or to discuss other matters of interest to the customer. The customer service function will be integrated to operations along with the corresponding procurement and scheduling function. This group will have the responsibility of ensuring that customer needs are met, and that all the elements are available that are needed for the production of the products to fill each customer request. The group will also have the responsibility of coordinating with the different cells to ensure that the appropriate priority is placed on customer orders.

As has been indicated, the quality function per se will not have direct responsibility for day-to-day activities. Rather, this responsibility will rest with the operations. Assuring that products are made in accordance with quality requirements will be the responsibility of the quality problem solving and assurance team. Bimonthly meetings will be held between customers and internal personnel assigned to evaluate the organization's performance. A quality assurance individual will be called upon, however, if an unusual event occurs. This person will be familiar with the product overall and how it functions as well as root cause problem solving and statistical techniques. Once the quality event is resolved and corrective procedures or techniques determined, operators will be thoroughly briefed so that a recurrence is avoided.

The ultimate lean organization also will be clearly oriented

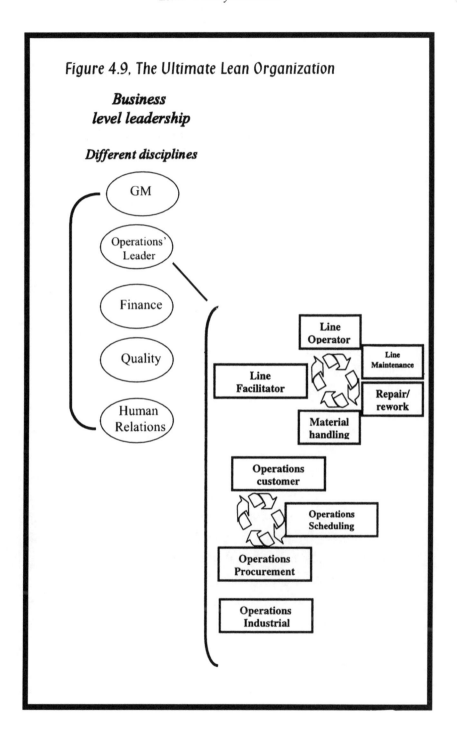

Figure 4.9, The Ultimate Lean Organization

toward achieving financial objectives. As part of this, product engineers will present their plans to manufacturing personnel to assure feasibility and ease of manufacturing. Functions such as facilities maintenance, shipping and local purchasing will be consolidated into a particular process organization at a location. The objective is to streamline, facilitate and to eliminate bureaucracy, muda, and non value added activities.

The human resources organization has an important role to play in this type of organization as well as in the transformation process. In the lean organization, a need exists to modify expectations, and evolve toward skill-based pay. This means not only that personnel will be rewarded in accordance with their skills but also that growth and rewards will be achieved through the development of a successful organization. Individuals will be able to take on more responsibility within their team and share in the team's success. But they must also realize that the number of management positions will be quite limited, if they exist at all.

Career development will need to be planned and discussed, and a path laid down. Individual growth will no longer happen by moving up the ladder of a hierarchy. Rather, it will come as a result of increased knowledge and skill, as well as the development of leadership qualities. The leaders of disciplines will not be part of a hierarchy, but rather, work as a team. The leaders of each operation, for example, will report directly to the general manager. They will be true leaders who represent their operation in a way similar to that of a congressional or parliamentary representative.

In some locations, there may not be an individual for every discipline. Each function needs to be covered, but some personnel will be multi skilled. This will be visible on the shop floor where a need will not exist for every production line to have a person for every discipline. Depending on the facility and the product, it may be possible for a team leader, as well as repair, maintenance, or material handling personnel to assist more than one line.

For this approach to work, personnel will be trained continuously in team building, lean enterprise, and interpersonal skills. Systems must be present, and continually improved for gathering, evaluating, reporting on, and implementing suggestions on ways to improve. Contributions made by individuals will be lauded, but financial incentives for individuals will not exist because these have a tendency to promote competition and discourage teamwork. Rather, incentive plans, if any, will encompass entire groups, or teams.

Human resources will have the responsibility of keeping a finger on the pulse of the company's culture and its commitment to a team approach as well as the employment of lean principles and practices. A method will be in place to keep personnel informed of these issues throughout the company. They will be discussed each week in strategy and implementation team meetings, where the question will be asked continually, "Is the company performing as a championship team?"

The physical layout of the ultimate lean enterprise will not be that of a traditional business, and it will not look like one. The number of offices will be limited in order to promote communication among individuals. Where offices exist, they will likely have transparent windows facing the interior of the building to further encourage the integration of personnel.

Fully equipped conference rooms will be available for use by teams. Video conferencing capabilities will facilitate the linking of the company's line personnel to customer personnel, and within larger organizations, to other facilities.

Lean enterprise techniques will be employed throughout. Continuous flow of value added activities rule the day, with no more inventory than five parts between operators. The same applies to office activities where a continuous review of information flows will be evaluated, and non value-added activities will be eliminated. Material handlers feed materials directly to workstations. Raw materials and components will be warehoused at the point of use, and will be handled solely by kanbans. Sourcing of them will be handled directly with suppliers, and control will be visual rather than accomplished through paper documents.

Inventory will be held to the minimum compatible with the volume of use, and the time required for replenishment. There will be no incoming inspection. Quality assurance will be handled by the vendor, or if necessary, it will take place in the manufacturing process.

Sourcing, customer service, and scheduling will work together as one team and will be integrated within the corresponding operation responsible for product manufacturing. One of the team members will be selected as the leader, and represent the group day-to-day with the operations leader.

Production information will be constantly updated and made available visually to line operators. Hourly production targets for each line will be determined based on customer needs. Line balancing will be performed by the operators themselves, and not by industrial engineering. Maintenance personnel will be assigned to specific lines and will be focused on ensuring that everything works properly allowing operators to meet customer needs. A quality reject analysis will be made on-line immediately upon the occurrence of such an event, and corrective action taken immediately to prevent its reoccurrence. All company resources provide support to and facilitate production.

Industrial and product engineering will be dedicated to a particular process organization. It will be their responsibility to serve the assembly lines by solving manufacturing problems, and they will be the ones who train line personnel when necessary.

Assembly lines will be manned by cells, or line teams. These will remain together in order to promote esprit d'corps, rather than pulled apart because of changes in shift requirements. When an individual must leave the line for any reason, he or she will be replaced by the team leader, or by a repair person, or material handler. (In some operations, a dedicated "jockey" may be required to fill in.)

Line leaders will be present continuously at assembly or production lines, and will not have an office or desk located away from the line. Their role will be dramatically different from the traditional role of a supervisor. They will reinforce interpersonal relationships among team members in order to promote a strong team effort, and a strong sense of solidarity. Their goal will be to build a team in which the group is more important than its individual components. Primarily, he or she will be a motivator. When required, this individual will replace an operator who may be temporarily absent. He or she may also fill in for others, such as repair personnel or material handlers. Team leaders also will be problem solvers who focus on enabling the team to meet hourly production objectives by calling on functions such as engineering, quality assurance, scheduling, and human resources. He or she will lead daily meetings and decide, with input from the team, on replacements for team members who may be out sick or on vacation. The team leader also will coordinate the implementation of suggested process improvements.

An organization such as the one described above will be vastly different than what most of us are accustomed to, and the ramifications are many. With the greatly magnified productivity such an organization will enjoy, with the increased job satisfaction it will provide workers, with its focus on customer needs and desires, and with the appreciation of shareholder value that most certainly will accrue, organizations such as this are almost certain to become the norm rather than the exception. This prediction may take many years to come to fruition. Nevertheless, we are convinced that all that needs to happen in an industry will be for one lean enterprise to become established. Competing businesses will be forced to follow.

Think of it. You may be the one to cause the transformation to begin in your industry.

## A Look Ahead

We believe that a profound revolution is gathering momentum in the world of business. While this is not limited to one country or to a particular industry, to date the significance of this revolution has been underrated by the financial community and the media. It is a move by businesses, particularly those in manufacturing, to adopt lean practices and techniques. The primary reason that it is underrated seems clear. Individuals highly knowledgeable in financial matters, and in general business practices, often have limited understanding of the processes of manufacturing and production. We suspect this because a general atmosphere of incredulousness appears to exist about the behavior of price indexes.

"How long," many wonder aloud, "can prices remain stable, or even fall, as business and employment continue to expand?" We believe the answer is, "For the foreseeable future."

Certainly, there will continue to be economic ups and downs. Bear markets will follow bull markets. Interest rates will rise and fall. Off years will follow good years. But we believe the long term outlook is excellent. An era of productivity gains is just beginning that will rival the twenty year period following World War II. Our own experience is that initial gains on the order of 25 to 40% in direct and indirect productivity are commonplace when an enterprise undergoes lean transformation. In addition, because the continuous striving for improvement is one of the underlying tenets of the lean enterprise, gains such as these are only the beginning. Toyota, which pioneered many lean enterprise techniques, has been at it since the end of the 1940s, yet still manages to realize productivity gains every year.

Whether your business is a small one filling a niche, or a worldwide leader in its category, it is our sincere hope that by conveying to you what we have learned, we will in some way further the success of your lean transformation. We believe that putting into practice what we have presented here will help to enhance the value of a business for its shareholders and investors, increase the effectiveness of management, improve the lives of workers, and help to ensure the continued growth of prosperity for society as a whole.

Keep the vision of your lean enterprise firmly in mind. Never turn from your goal. Begin, and soon the work will be done.

# End Notes

1. Money Magazine, March 1996 issue, pages 134-137.
2. Money Magazine, March 1997 issue, page 144.
3. USA Today, July 17, 1997, "GM, Ford show profit despite labor, sales woes."
4. Eiji Toyoda was a second generation descendent of the founders of Toyota. According to information provided in the book by James P. Womack, Daniel T. Jones and Daniel Roos, *The Machine that Changed the World*, Harper Perennial, 1990, the family name "Toyoda" means "abundant rice field" in Japanese. The name of the company, Toyota, has no meaning and was selected as the winner of a contest to name the company held in 1936.
5. August 1997, just prior to a two for one split.
6. Facts concerning the Dell Computer case history related here are from two magazine articles: Businessweek, *April 7*, 1997, "Whirlwind on the Web," and 'Techno File/The Trends and Products That Drive the: No Big Deal Why Michael Dell Isn't Afraid of the New Compaq," Fortune Magazine, March 2, 1998.
7. In order to become fully lean, Dell will need to require that lean practices be adopted throughout its supply chain as in the case of Toyota.
8. Businessweek, April 7, 1997, "Whirlwind on the Web."
9. Ibid.
10. Richmond Times-Dispatch, August 25,1997, Associate Press article headed "Detroit puts car shopping online."
11. *Built to Last*, copyright 1994 and 1997 by James C. Collins and Jerry Porras, paperback edition, HarperBusiness, Page 82.
12. Ibid.
13. Ibid.
14. Ibid.
15. Ibid.
16. Ibid, page 83.
17. *And I Quote*, copyright 1992 by Ashton Applewhite, William R. Evan, III, and Andrew Frothingham. St. Martin's Press, page 69.
18. *Bullseyes & Blunders, Stories or Business Success & Failure* by Robert F. Hartley, pages 217-226, published by John Wiley & Sons, Inc. New York, New York, 1987.
19. *The 1997 Yankelovich Monitor*, Yankelovich and Partners, 1997.
20. Fortune Magazine, "How Toyota Defies," December 8, 1997.
21. Ibid.
22. Authors of *The Machine That Changed the World* (with Daniel Roos) and *Lean Thinking*.
23. Our editor, Stephen Hawley Martin, studied the effects of advertising frequency over the period from 1979 through 1986 while at The Martin Agency. He has written a number of articles on this subject that appeared in the trade publication, *Marketing & Media Decisions*.
24. *The Seven Habits of Highly Effective People*, Copyright 1989 by Stephen R. Covey, Simon & Schuster, New York.
25. *Don't Sweat the Small Stuff . . . and It's all Small Stuff*, by Richard Carlson, PH.D, Copyright 1997, Hyperion, New York.
26. "Yield" refers to the percentage of good parts produced by a given process.
27. January 27, 1998

# Appendix

A series of questions appear on the following pages that you and others in your organization can use to determine the areas of the business that need the most effort to lift them to the standard of a lean enterprise. Have members of your lean conversion team answer them now, and then again at regular intervals, such as every six months. You'll see where progress is being made, and be in position to make mid course corrections toward becoming an organization that is fully lean.

## 1. Workplace safety, Order and Cleanliness

| | Valuation Factors 1 | Valuation Factors 6 | Valuation Factors 10 | Valuation Comments | Valuation Rating |
|---|---|---|---|---|---|
| **Safety** | Unsafe; many hazards; policies loosely enforced; local ordinances violated | Moderately safe; few hazards; policies enforced somewhat; general local ordinance compliance | Very safe; no hazards; rigid adherence to policies; full local ordinance compliance | | |
| **Lighting/ Brightness** | Poorly lit; dingy; looks like a cave; factory and offices have not been painted for 10 years | Moderately lit; some fresh painting in offices and factory, ceilings, walls, floors, machines | Brightly lit, like daylight; freshly painted ceilings, walls, floors, machines | | |
| **Cleanliness** | Very dirty; floors not clean; dust/oil on machinery; office desks, chairs; file cabinets deteriorated | Generally clean, but not immaculate; floors, machines, offices somewhat dirty; equipment deteriorated; some cleaning at end of shift | Offices/factory immaculately clean; no dust/oil on machines; no debris or dirt; you can eat off the floor; cleaning at end of shift | | |
| **Order** | Very cluttered; lots of junk in aisles and work areas; disorganized desks, files and cabinets | Generally uncluttered; limited junk in aisles and work areas, including offices; some use of marking systems | Only critical items on shop floor, offices and work areas; clear markings for all items on floors (e.g. Kanban squares); use of shadow boards for tools | | |
| **Overall** | Pig Sty | Ok, but not great | Looks like a hospital | | |

## 2. Just in Time Production

| | Valuation Factors | | | Valuation Comments | Valuation Rating |
|---|---|---|---|---|---|
| | 1 | 6 | 10 | | |
| **Continous Flow Manufacturing** | Disjointed operations; colonies of machines; large batches | Some processes in continuous flow | High degree of continuous flow, small batch sizes for remaining batch processes | | |
| **Pull Scheduling** | No Pull scheduling; heavy MRPI use; build to forecast philosophy | Some use of Pull scheduling via Kanban system shop floor, system not linked to customer or supplier; primarily build to forecast | Full Kanban use from customer order through suppliers; MRPI only for planning and long lead release; build only to customer demand | | |
| **Line Change-over; Machine Setup** | Long hours | Some short changeovers (minutes); some long | Assembly line changeover in one takt time; batch change over in less than ten minutes | | |
| **Total Productive Maintenance** | None. "Fix it when it breaks." | Some implemention of TPM | Full implemention of TPM program | | |
| **Overall** | Mass producer | In between | True Lean producer | | |

## 3. Six Sigma quality built into the product and the process.

| | Valuation Factors | | | Valuation Comments | Valuation Rating |
|---|---|---|---|---|---|
| | 1 | 6 | 10 | | |
| **Six sigma targets are part of the design process** | No | Partial use of design and process FMEA; six sigma objectives sometimes are used as design objectives | Full use of design and process FMEA; six sigma objectives are clearly used as design objectives | | |
| **Equipment design to detect defects and stop production** | None | Some machines have self-stop capability | All machines stop automatically when defects are detected | | |
| **Operators' authority to stop production for quality defects** | None | Operators have authority, but use it sporadically | Operators have authority and responsbility to stop line; individual quality responsibility is fully internalized | | |
| **Mistake proofing to prevent defects** | None | Partial implementation for critical processes | Full implementation on all critical processes | | |
| **FIFO inventory control** | None | Partial | Rigidly adhered to; easy to use (for example flow-through racks) | | |

## 3. Six Sigma quality built into the product and the process (continuation)

| | Valuation Factors | | | Valuation Comments | Valuation Rating |
|---|---|---|---|---|---|
| | 1 | 6 | 10 | | |
| **Close loop quality problem resolution** | None | Some quality problems logged, prioritized and assigned a team to fix it | All quality problems logged, prioritized and assigned a team to fix it | | |
| **Root-cause problem solving** | Rare. Fixing quality problems is not a priority. | Sporadic. Problem solving stops at easiest solution, not necessarily correct solution. | Rigorous use of five whys; key person trained in problem-solving methods | | |
| **Use of SPC** | None | Approximately 50% of key processes control to six sigma levels | All key processes controlled to six sigma levels | | |
| **Standardized work** | No work standards or instructions; strictly on-the-job-training | Approximately 50% implementation of standardized work and visual work instructions | Work methods fully standardized and clearly identified by visual methods (i.e. 3D drawings) | | |
| **Incoming products and materials quality** | No self-certified suppliers | Some suppliers are self-certified and consistent quality is experienced | All key suppliers are self-certified and supply consistently agreed-upon quality products | | |
| **Overall** | Questionable quality | Average quality | Six sigma producer | | |

## 4. Empowered teams

| | Valuation Factors | | | Valuation Comments | Valuation Rating |
|---|---|---|---|---|---|
| | 1 | 6 | 10 | | |
| **Autocratic versus participative management** | Autocratic; "theory X" management style | Mixed autocratic and participative management style | Participative management style with strong employee input and strong top manager leadership | | |
| **Levels of hierarchy** | Highly layered and hierarchal (i.e. four or more management levels between GM and shop floor) | In between | Flat organization, structured in accordance with the LE facility structures as defined by SC (only two levels; no managerial structures) | | |
| **Self-directed work teams** | None | Some implementation of self directed teams | Operators have authority and responsibility to stop line; individual quality responsibility is fully internalized | | |
| **Team empowerment** | None | Some, but largely in name only | High degree of team empowerment to make key decisions | | |
| **Overall** | Traditional, autocratic | Transitioning to team environment | Full implementation of empowered teams; real LE facility | | |

## 5. Visual management

| | 1 | Valuation Factors 6 | 10 | Valuation Comments | Valuation Rating |
|---|---|---|---|---|---|
| **Visual performance charts** | None, management by computer reports, key performance data only available to a select few | Some use of visual display techniques; key performance data available to certain levels | Clear visual display of company performance (centrally) and team performances (at work cells and offices) | | |
| **Warehouse inventory control** | Inventory in "random access" warehouse; only computer knows where it is; no visual control | Approximate implementation of visual inventory management | Inventory in fixed locations with clear min/max indicators of visual control | | |
| **Shop floor WIP inventory control** | Minimal visual control, inventory stacked in work stations in random order | Approximately 50% implementation of shop floor WIP visual control | Clear fixed location identification with FIFO control; Kanban squares used for WIP located on floor | | |
| **Use of visual charts** | None | Approximately 50% of the facility personel use visual charts to manage their daily activities | Operators and office personnel use factory and office visual charts to manage their daily activities and performances | | |
| **Visual indicators update** | Seldom updates | Some updates weekly or monthly, implemented by management | Operators and office personnel update charts and visual information display continuously | | |
| **Overall** | Traditional company information management | In between | Fully visual company | | |

## 6. Continuous Pursuit of Perfection

| | Valuation Factors | | | Valuation Comments | Valuation Rating |
|---|---|---|---|---|---|
| | 1 | 6 | 10 | | |
| **Process for change implementation** | None | Process is in place but each request has to "get in line;" occasional response to requests (only when we have time) | All company organizations available and respond rapidly to changes and request for support; responses within 48 hours | | |
| **Change implementation** | Only when designed by engineering and approved by management | Approximate implementation of visual inventory management | Operators and office personnel have the authority and the responsibility to implement changes | | |
| **Operators and office personnel meetings** | Occasionally (once or twice a month) | Some implementation of information meetings but not systematic and widespread | Meetings are held every day for 10 minutes and once a week for half an hour | | |
| **Continuous improvement team** | None | Some, but largely in name only, limited empowerment to realize changes | Large number of teams which follow established rules, with clearly measurable improvement results attained in short periods of time | | |
| **Waste culture (muda)** | None | Some actions present but no clear culture of managing and eliminating waste | Fully committed to eliminating waste | | |
| **Overall** | Talk the talk but do not walk the talk | In between | Full walking the talk; a true LE environment | | |

## 7. Overall company organization and management style

| | Valuation Factors | | | Valuation Comments | Valuation Rating |
|---|---|---|---|---|---|
| | 1 | 6 | 10 | | |
| **Company structure** | Divided in different departments | Some integration between departments but still functionally divided | Fully integrated into a single company, with no departments; organized as in the LE facility with two management levels and with fully integrated disciplines | | |
| **Compensation base** | By seniority management position | In between | Skill-based pay | | |
| **Office layout** | Managers have their offices, which are enclosed and with limited access by lower rank employees | In between | All offices have transparent glass; limited offices and people meet in glass-enclosed conference rooms; everyone can access everyone else | | |
| **Leadership style** | Fully hierarchal and authoritative; "finding the guilty one approach;" people fearful of the higher levels | In transition | Leaders become motivators, coaches, trainers; problem-solving approach; focus on training for problem solving | | |
| **Communications** | Highly bureaucratic and only limited to few; holding information is an indication of power | Some information available at different levels; limited information of actions presented in a timely manner | Open communications about company issues with information flowing freely to, and from, everyone | | |
| **Overall** | Traditional company | In between | LE company | | |

8. Company services

| | Valuation Factors | | | Valuation | Valuation Rating |
|---|---|---|---|---|---|
| | 1 | 6 | 10 | | |
| **Purchasing approach** | Suppliers are treated as enemies | In between | Full involement and integration with company objectives and strategies | | |
| **Purchasing policies and practices** | Full use of MRPI paper driven; no visual indications | Kanban implemented with 50% of suppliers; paper control and tracking | Kanban driven; visual indications with minimal paper control | | |
| **Purchasing operating practices** | An independent organization in continuous conflict with manufacturing and other functions | In between | Part of the operations organization and integrated in its functioning | | |
| **Human Resources** | Totally traditional in a staff role | In between | Fully aware of the pulse of the company; suggesting training and communications as required to bring culture to a lean enviroment | | |
| **Human Resource training** | None or limited | Some training but limited in scope and duration | Extensive training on Lean approaches, empowerment and coaching; at least 80 hours of training per employee annum, measurement of achievements | | |
| **Human Resources Personal evaluations** | Done exclusively by upper management limited feedback; | In between | 360-degrees approach at all levels with continuous support for personal and professional growth and job satisfaction | | |

## 8. Company services (continuation)

| | Valuation Factors | | | Valuation Comments | Valuation Rating |
|---|---|---|---|---|---|
| | 1 | 6 | 10 | | |
| **Product Engineering** | Not hearing the voice of the customer; new product designs taking more than a year; disconnected from production considerations | Limited customer participation; new product designs taking more than six months; some considerations and quality needs | Design with client, quality, manufacturing, sales, purchasing; new product designs in six months or less; design for manufacturability | | |
| **Manufacturing Process Engineering** | Designing machinery large lot sizes; long setup times; most of the time in the offices; limited knowledge of processes and products | In between | Designing machinery for flow and not for capacity; fully present in the factory floor, full knowledge of processes and products | | |
| **Scheduling, Customer Service** | Traditional separate functions; MRPI driven | Separate functions; no direct flow between order entry and shop floor; Kanban control made by scheduler | Fully integrated into a single organization; one hour between order enry and order in shop floor; scheduling done at cell level | | |
| **Finance and Administration** | Fully traditional standard costing; taking several days for monthly closing, not integrated with the rest of the functions | In between | Monthly closing in one day, information; metrics availible in support of shop floor; performance measurement to support LE environments | | |
| **Overall** | Traditional company | In between | LE company | | |

# Lean Assessment Chart

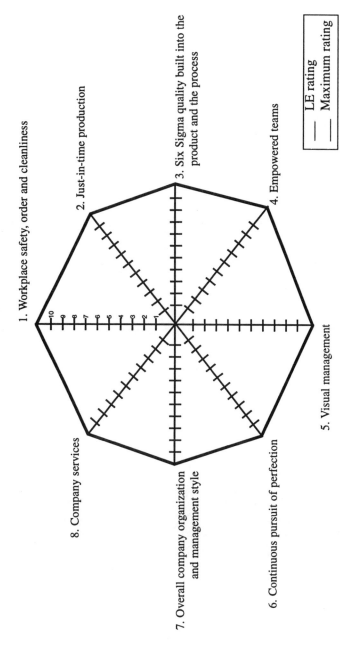

1. Workplace safety, order and cleanliness
2. Just-in-time production
3. Six Sigma quality built into the product and the process
4. Empowered teams
5. Visual management
6. Continuous pursuit of perfection
7. Overall company organization and management style
8. Company services

LE rating
Maximum rating